MIND
AND
THE INTELLECT

COLLECTED TALKS
VOLUME I

MARGARET JOHNSON

Edited by
Laurie Parker

I-Level
Mystics of the World, Publisher
Longboat Key, Florida

TABLE OF CONTENTS

FOREWORD

MARGARET JOHNSON (MEG) was my spiritual guide and teacher for seventeen years in this parenthesis. Although she made her transition in 2011, her presence and love continue to be felt daily.

Meg was not only one of the most loving individuals ever experienced in my lifetime but also a strict disciplinarian who kept pounding on me until I caught the spiritual principle she was striving to convey, then having me recognize and finally realize its importance. She taught enlightenment was not difficult if I could simply work on the requirements necessary to achieve it. Those requirements were the continual practice of:

1. Ensuring my focus and gratitude were always on the One.
2. Studying, learning and comprehending the universal Spiritual principles of Life .
3. Meditating to allow these spiritual principles to enter into and purify consciousness (dropping from my head to my heart).
4. Putting these principles continually into practice.
5. Exercising and then expressing these principles through constant sharing ("Service to God through service to others").

Meg was not a teacher who traveled around the world or even around the country as she wanted to work closely on a one-on-one level with around twenty-five individuals. She would spend intensive and focused time with each student, bringing us into an awareness of the ever more powerful possibilities derived through a group consciousness, proving the power and majesty of what this level of consciousness can demonstrate.

When I had a problem, Meg took it upon herself to work with me to recognize the illusion posing as the problem, followed by uncovering the principle necessary to dissolve it. While several of these challenges, later to be perceived as opportunities, came during my spiritual relationship with Meg, none were larger than that experienced in the 2007/2008 financial crisis.

One of my business roles had been to assist friends and very close family members in their financial and investment planning. This was really an outgrowth from my previous professional activities of investing in private and public companies. For over twenty-five years, I was asked to manage and oversee the investments and savings of many members of my family, business associates and close friends. Among those were my mother, wife, children, uncles, aunts, cousins, business associates, and others. Even Meg asked if I would oversee her life savings.

In 2007, in what was later discovered to be fraudulent activities by those who had been trusted for many years (somewhat similar to Bernie Madoff), I found over 80% of the funds entrusted to them by me had vanished. Additionally, all of my personal net worth, built over the previous 25 years was wiped out. It was my worst nightmare imaginable. I felt humiliated beyond belief.

When this was explained to close friends, family members, and others, many were indignant and felt I had defrauded them. Not only had I lost my fortune but they had lost theirs, believing I was personally responsible. I became incredibly depressed, despondent, and bordering on thoughts of suicide. At least through dying, the small amount of life insurance from policies still maintained would be available to provide some small recovery from the significant amounts of funds lost.

Nervously, the time came for me to share what had transpired with Meg, explaining her life savings were virtually gone. It was absolutely unbelievable what she said to me. Without a trace of personal reaction or loss, she immediately responded, "Well then, it's time to get to work. What is the spiritual principle required to be recognized and ultimately realized in this appearance? Go deeper and find the principle underlying this apparent problem and work with it." "Apparent problem"—what, are you kidding me?

Back up a moment. When I needed to let Meg know what had happened, her doctors had recently suggested she had a limited time to live. If her first response was unbelievable, her second response was unfathomable. She continued, "I'm not going anywhere until we get this taken care of, as this is a tremendous opportunity for you." Opportunity?? Finally, the rubber had hit the road. This was no longer about intellectualizing what these principles could do in my life; it was time to prove them.

Meg stood with me day after day for over two years, expecting me to check in daily as she guided and instructed me each step of the way in free-flowing Love. I never felt an inkling of judgment, criticism, or condemnation. She was living all she had taught and I became the fortunate recipient and beneficiary of this tsunami of love and grace.

Now let's do the math. After being personally wiped out and only having about 20% of the original amount invested by others who had trusted me to conservatively oversee and invest, I went to each individual and said, "I'm not sure how this will happen, but I am going to pay back every penny you entrusted with me at a rate of 2% per month. Therefore, you will be paid in total in about four years. If I can't do that, then I will die trying." I honestly meant and felt this, based upon the life insurance proceeds that would be forthcoming.

Well, the principles for me were threefold. The first was "What have ye in the house?" (the Golden Rule for Meg) and the second: "Begin to pour." And finally, "to die to my personal sense of self." Humanly, there was nothing more I would have loved to do at that time.

What then happened is something usually reserved for fairy tales. While miraculously being able to pay 2% per month to everyone (remember, each month's payment represented 10% of my initial starting capital), after two years and four months everyone was paid in full. Grace truly had taken over my life.

Once I let Meg know this was now possible, she said "Good, this has been a great learning experience for you." Two weeks later Meg made her transition, living over two years longer than the doctors told her she could. Obviously, she did not pay much attention to them as working with her students and proving the principles were far more important to her.

The above story represents the most miserable, unbelievable, exhilarating, learning experience in my life. What else can be said? All I can say is this was a classic example of Meg, her teaching and her love: she was an absolute giant in my life.

Michael Krupp
Longboat Key, Florida

INTRODUCTION

IN 1994, MARGARET JOHNSON along with the many students who formed The Atlanta Study Center in Atlanta, Georgia, hosted the first of what was to be a bi-annual series of classes based on the teachings of Joel Goldsmith.* By this time, this group of dedicated individuals had been meeting together for over twenty years but had stayed "underground"; that is to say, they practiced and studied as a private group under the guidance of Meg, not traveling widely or hosting others.

I met Meg, as she liked to be called, by happenstance in the early 1990s. I had moved to Washington State with my two daughters after having lived in Albuquerque, New Mexico for 23 years. At the time of the move, I was handling the tape recordings of another gifted teacher of Joel's message and though the move involved a huge transition for me and my family, I was able to manage the orders that came in for this activity.

One day, I received a letter from a woman in Atlanta, ordering not one class of perhaps four talks, but ten copies of one class of four talks! I had no equipment so was taking orders and having them processed nearby and then would create labels and ship the cassettes out. Needless to say, this sudden avalanche of orders took me aback and created challenges at the same time. "That must be some group in Atlanta," I told myself. I wrote Meg asking naively if she had

---

* Joel Goldsmith (1892 – 1964), an internationally recognized spiritual teacher, author, and healer, taught a mystical message based on spiritual principles revealed to him. He called this message "The Infinite Way."

a tape group. "Yes," she wrote back. Later another query: "Do you also have group work?" "Yes" was the answer. Later, "Do you also teach?" "Yes."

It took two or three months of correspondence before I gradually learned that Meg indeed had a tape group and also gave weekly classes and more: Her interest in the materials I was sending out—classes related to new expressions in group work—was precisely the result of what was opening up in their very active Study Center. With over twenty years of dedicated work, their group consciousness was unfolding in ways that were coming into active expression. It was a privilege and joy to be able to attend some of the early workshops being conducted by Meg's students at the Center and also attend one or two of the weekly classes that she presented.

In 1994, the Center hosted the first of a series of classes to those outside of the group who were interested in The Infinite Way message. That opened up their private work to a wider audience. What you will find within these pages are very minimally edited transcripts of both the April Hotel Classes as well as the October Study Center Classes of 1994.

The April series, in essence, introduces the Atlanta group and describes the way Spirit was being expressed in their ongoing classes and workshops. The April sessions also emphasize Meg's way of working with the fundamentals of The Infinite Way principles.

In the October classes, Meg presents two very important threads in her teaching: Mind and the Intellect and Supply. She states in a class on spiritual supply:

> *Now spiritual supply is spiritual discernment, spiritual discernment of a spiritual principle. It has nothing whatever to do with our intellectual concepts of supply. Our intellectual*

concepts are what form in the mind when consciousness realizes and discerns the principle of spiritual supply.

So here we have Consciousness creates, mind forms, and the conditioned intellect interprets that to us in whatever way our human need seems to be. Let's say we have a lack of some kind and we go within to discern the principle, what I call "going for the principle"; let's bypass all the concepts and go for the principle. What is supply? In reality, what is supply? You know what its forms are, and that again is the flesh that is here today and gone tomorrow. What we want, though, is permanent supply. We don't want a bank account today and barrenness next week. We want a consciousness of supply; we want to know the principle behind supply. So, we go for that principle.

Here she presents the golden key: *"...we go for that principle."* Throughout these classes, and in fact, throughout all of Margaret's teaching, is that foundation—"going for the principle"—setting that firm, unmoving ground of not just knowing the principle, but experiencing and being it.

In the spirit of wholehearted dedication to The Infinite Way principles, these transcripts illuminate one teacher's and one group's dedicated consciousness, and the beautiful outward form it took as classwork, group expression and individual freedom.

Laurie Parker
Boise, Idaho

What Have Ye In the House?

GOOD EVENING. I'm very grateful to you who have come such long distances to share in our celebration, our emancipation, of the Atlanta Study Center. For over 20 years, we have worked sacredly and silently building a group consciousness, and except for one of our new students who spilled the beans and exposed us, we would still be in the closet of The Infinite Way. However, God works in mysterious ways so here we are, happy to be free at last and out of the closet.

When we first began this activity so many years ago, there were five students; we opened the Study Center and within a few weeks we had to expand our quarters and rent an additional space. A few weeks after that, or I'd say two months after that, we had students who were sitting on the floor and we had to expand again. Up until about two years ago, with the exception of about three or four first-generation Infinite Way students, this group had never attended a major Infinite Way class. Early on, we sponsored one or two classes here in Atlanta which were well attended and were a wonderful experience. I then took some of the students to major classwork in different parts of the country and felt that that was the way a study center should be operated: we work twice a week, three times a week, and then on the occasion of major classwork, we would all get on the airplane and go attend these classes and then come back in the same state of consciousness and do it all over again.

The students, though, wouldn't have it. One day they came to me and said, "It just doesn't seem practical that we are spending all of this money traveling to these major classes and all of this time listening to other teachers, when we feel we have the best of it here at home and we would prefer to put our time and our energy and our monetary support into our own study center and develop it." So, I acceded to that and that's really when our group activity began.

Now over the years, and those of you who have groups or who will be starting groups will discover this, everyone who comes to you is not really a serious, loyal, and dedicated student. Those qualities, which are spiritual qualities, must be drawn out of the student the same as integrity, the same as conviction, the same as the Spirit itself. Ways have to be opened up for the imprisoned splendor to escape and some students who genuinely think that their interest is in a teaching as sacrosanct as the spiritual teaching of The Infinite Way, quickly find that they cannot take the discipline. Our work over these years has consisted of discipline, discipline, discipline; practice, practice, practice; plod, plod, plod with some joys and delights along the way. Therefore, it is a tribute to this student body that although we have complained, we have griped, we have fallen down, and we have fallen away, we have always come back.

In the beginning, we had many more students and for years they were in and out. Finally, about fifteen years ago there seemed to be a settling into a certain number, a core group, here in Atlanta who seemed to suddenly catch the vision and it was like a leap upward in consciousness and there was a sort of settling into the serious business of being "on the way."

Up until then, it was a kind of catch-as-catch-can. When that leap happened, we began one-on-one work of a very intense nature. Our schedule, to use a Southern expression, is strong enough to choke a horse. You would not believe what these students have been subjected to. I don't believe what I have subjected them to, and myself along the way. I always hear Joel's voice in the background and it is like cracking the whip in my consciousness. They used to call me, and they may still behind my back, "the sword swinging Christ." (Well, I always felt that I was the Southern Christ.) But this is the way it had come to me when I received my instruction to move to Atlanta and establish a real Infinite Way activity, a strong Infinite Way study center. Joel had impressed me very much with his talks about study centers and his vision of study centers in The Infinite Way and this was my interpretation.

Begin to Pour

When we grew or drew together as a nucleus, the real work began; the problems began to arise also. The first principle that we took on to demonstrate was the principle of spiritual supply. Now of course in those days, nobody thought supply was spiritual; actually, everybody was broke, myself included, and that's why we had to take up the principle of supply. We have learned over the years that the manna falls day by day, but in the beginning, because of the claim in the group consciousness of lack, we began our work with that principle and for many years that was the main principle of our group work. Today, I can safely say that this group has demonstrated not only material supply, but a great outpouring of spiritual supply, which is the ultimate demonstration of that principle.

We found along the way that many gifts of the Spirit take infinite form: supply really is outgo not income, and it begins within oneself. Every day, we search ourselves to see "What do I have in the house today? What can I share today?" Everyone has a talent, everyone has a spiritual gift; even a gift of gab is a spiritual gift, a sense of humor is a spiritual gift, the ability to read well is a spiritual gift, poetry, yet we never think of these as spiritual gifts. We think of spiritual gifts as healing the sick or raising the dead; of course, these are the ultimate spiritual gifts but we don't have those yet, we can't raise the dead yet. So, we need to start where we are in consciousness. "What do I have in the house, now? Today? A loaf of bread? A garment hanging in the closet I haven't worn? An hour I can spend with an ailing senior citizen? A dog I can take on a walk for a friend?" There are millions of ways in which we can begin to pour.

Now of course I know that those in this group here tonight have all been in The Infinite Way for some time—many years—and you don't need to be told that. But do you know, every morning when I wake up, I still go within to find out "What do I have in the house today? What can I share today?" The other day when I was under pressure preparing for this class, my husband who is a very dear man and very support-ive of this work, scheduled a new fence to be built, yard work for my housekeeper, and an inspection by the termite control people, and cleaning of the ducts in our house for Monday and Tuesday of this week. Well, very unlike me, I became irritated [laughter], and said to him, "This is a very bad time for you to schedule all this work because I have a lot to do this week," and he, knowing that he just didn't think, was defensive and said, "Well, I will take care of it." And of course I said, "You bet your life, you will," went upstairs and went into meditation. In meditation, immediately I heard, "I will take care of it. *I* will take care of it." And I thought, "How many times a day does God speak to us and we don't hear it?" Of course, *I* was going to take care of it, and my husband was telling me that. Now I don't often think of my husband as a very spiritual person, but there it was. "I will take care of it." And *I* did. I went to the study center Monday and Tuesday and had beautifully productive days and *I* took care of all those chores and they were done.

Now, if we don't respect and honor the *I* of people who don't have this wonderful advantage of a spiritual teaching, or this wonderful consciousness that is developed in us over the years, if we don't respect and honor their *I*, how are they ever going to open out a way for their imprisoned splendor to escape? Most of the time we are so busy passing judgment and imposing our own concepts of good and evil on the faces of the people close to us that we block the flow that was meant for us. The bread we cast upon the waters is literally earmarked for us, for whatever we have in the house, whether it is an explosion of anger or whether it is a blessing of peace, is earmarked to return to us.

Now the principle of supply is Omnipresence. If we could just glimpse that alone, we would have the entire teaching, we would be almost home. If we could see that there is really only One, that the I that *I* am is you and the I that you are is me, and whatever I do unto you, I am doing unto myself, then we would know what the principle of supply is. When I give to you, whatever I give to you, it is like passing it from my right hand to my left, and it comes back to me from my left hand to my right. There is no other way. There is one Infinite Way principle, one Power, one Intelligence, and *I* am that. And it is equally true when *you* declare that.

If, at this stage of our development, we don't want to accept that, then we are still held in bondage. So tonight, we are bearing witness to the truth of being and the acceptance of that truth which is our next step on the path. It was never meant that a handful of teachers were to serve the world. The function of a teacher is to bring individual students into the realization of their own Godhood. I am that *I Am*. And students will grasp that in the measure that they begin to practice pouring and begin to practice sharing: "What have I in the house? What can I share?" The widow and her little mite poured, and it multiplied, it expanded.

The greatest gift that I have ever received was that instruction to begin to establish a real Infinite Way activity. When I started I didn't know much. Oh, I was well versed in the metaphysics; I could tell you what sentence was in what paragraph on what page in every book; I could quote to you extensively from all of the tapes; I knew all of the major teachers and many of the students; all of that was in my consciousness. Also, my mind had been purified with truth. But I had not experienced all of that truth. I had to start with what I had. "What have I in the house?"

Saying Yes

It is naïve to think that this work is going to bring you happiness. Joel never taught us that. He told us if we could say "no," to do so. But I could never say "no." It was "yes" from the beginning. When I came into The Infinite Way, I was living a normal life, with a nice family, living in a nice house, with a decent income: the American dream. I had no needs or desires that were overwhelming to me. No ambition. But I was miserable. There was something in me just screaming, "Is this all there is? There has to be more than this. If this is the best of human life, then I don't want it." I was fulfilled as a wife and mother, I'd been in business for years and risen to the top of my profession, and it just wasn't enough. But I didn't know where to look. I had abandoned orthodox religion years before because it was stagnant to me and I knew little or no metaphysics; all I'd ever studied was Dr. Fox.[*] Yet something was drawing me deeper and deeper within and I was screaming inside. Then one day the postman brought me a package and when I took it from his hand, I was shaking. I opened it and there was the book, *Practicing the Presence*.[**] It was a Saturday, the family was at home, and I was in the midst of vacuuming the living room floor. I sat down in the living room, left the vacuum cleaner and didn't get up until I had completed that book. When I did, I went directly to my desk, wrote a letter to Joel (his address was in the back of it) asking him to accept me as a student. I knew I had come home. There was never a doubt in my mind. He wrote back immediately, and his first words were "Welcome to my spiritual household."

So, from that point on it was "yes" all the way to me. That first generation of students went through a lot. All of us had obstacles and human responsibilities. None of us had any money. One of us would buy a tape and we would send it all around the country, lending it to each other. We lived just to receive Joel's letters, to go to his classes when we could, and hopefully to dispel our obstacles. It was not an easy time. If

---

[*] Emmet Fox (1886-1951) was a noted New Thought teacher of the 20th Century.

[**] Joel S. Goldsmith, *Practicing the Presence* (Longboat Key, FL : Acropolis Books).

Editor's note: All books and pamphlets by Joel S. Goldsmith listed in this book are available through www.acropolisbooks.com.

you have been in The Infinite Way for many years and you know some of the older students, you know that they were pioneers and that they made the way easier for the generation that came after. When I think of what Joel endured to bring this teaching into the world, and what his loyal co-workers did to introduce it into human consciousness—the writing, the editing, the traveling, the sacrificing—I am so grateful that by the time I came along, my way was easier. And today your way is easier because of all that. But because your way is easier, it is your responsibility now to make it easier for the next generation.

The Group Consciousness

In my unfoldment on group consciousness, it came to me that for so long a time illumination has been possible only one by one or only to the individual. But after over twenty years of working with a group and having them molded to a single unit, I see that the day is coming, if it is not already here, where a group consciousness of oneness can pass into illumination instead of one by one.

Now The Infinite Way work keeps unfolding. Many of us in my generation don't care for the change, we would like to keep it the same as it was. That is not possible. Joel never meant it to be that way. One of the things that has happened in our group work and in our study center over the last three years is that the older students—and by that I don't mean in chronological years—those who have been in The Infinite Way longer, have become a group doing world work. We meet every day for meditation, they have a workshop once a month and they have done some extraordinary healing work for the community, the student body, and for the world. The other group, the younger generation, those who have not been in

The Infinite Way that long, formed into a business and professional group* and you have only to talk to them to discover what strides have been made in the unfoldment of spiritual consciousness as far as they are concerned. They have learned (and we have tapes of recorded workshops from this group) to bring these principles into their everyday lives.

For so many years, in my generation, everyone thought that business was not a spiritual activity. People quit jobs thinking "This is not a spiritual activity and I am violating my spiritual integrity by staying in the marketplace." Well, we have been taught that we bloom where we are planted, that we bring these principles into the marketplace to spiritualize the marketplace. And as students have taken on the responsibility to go as a blessing into their place of business, they have seen wonderful demonstrations, sometimes almost miraculous events take place, as changes are made. So as the unfolding consciousness of The Infinite Way is now spreading in business, in the professions, in government, we have to stay in the city until we are called from on High; we bring the high calling to the city.

This is the aim of our group work and our group consciousness. We have educators, we have lawyers, we have teachers, we have supervisors, we have leaders. I cannot express the joy, the respect, that I feel in their experiences, and the fulfillment they have brought to me. The work they do is tremendous.

Now, this is what they are today. Fifteen years ago, well, what they were I really would not care to tell you [laughter]. You wouldn't believe it, not to see them today and to see the changes that have been wrought. But always, in their consciousness, there was that little bud ready to open, ready to

---

* A group dedicated to creativity and the arts was added as well.

bloom. I had to understand, and they had to understand too, that teachers only attract those students on their own vibration and students only attract a teacher on their own vibration and so we had to live with each other. I can remember telling them, "Don't blame it on me, I'm the teacher of your own consciousness."

Anyway, we are now at a point in our development where we are ready not only to be exposed and emancipated from our secret hideaway, but we are ready to share the trials and tribulations and the joys and the experience that we have had as a group. We would like so much to open our house to pour and share with anyone who would partake of our gifts of the Spirit which are multitudinous. It is to that end that we decided to give this class and invite those who are interested in a group activity. As I said, I feel this is the wave of the future, and other long-time Infinite Way students are feeling that way as well.

The days of traveling around from class to class, from teacher to teacher, I think are dwindling. But the day of reckoning is here where each one of us is taking our own individual responsibility to begin to pour and to draw our own unto us. It is to that end, we want to help. We have done it, we have experienced it, and we are not proselytizing it, we are just overwhelmed with the fact that it has now been recognized. We never intended it to be, we never showed it forth. But it was found out, and it is true, you cannot hide your light under a bushel.

Now, this is the work that was given me to do: to establish a group consciousness of oneness. It is a day in day out way of life. We are at the study center five days a week. We have a noon meditation every day, and some students come across town from downtown to make that noonday meditation. I have private one-on-one appointments three days a week, where students come in rotation for private instruction. We have Joel's tape work on Monday night; we are there for hours on Tuesday, on Wednesday the practitioner's group meets, and Wednesday night we have classwork; Thursday we have the noon meditation and three hours more if needed for appointments—one-on-one classwork—Friday the same thing. Saturdays all of us meditate at noon wherever we are and Sundays we give to our families and to relaxation.

This is a way of life for us. It is not a class on a busy weekend where we are lifted to a beautiful euphoric state of consciousness and perhaps one week later we are down in the dumps again; this is day in and day out, keeping our consciousness clear and free, keeping our minds stayed on truth, letting nothing enter to defile that truth and when something slips in, being quick to pick ourselves up and carry on. We have been disciplined, honed, as a group to come when called.

When the Persian Gulf War was on, these students were at the study center every day at noon for meditation, all of them, every day until that war was dissolved. Now this is world work. But you cannot expect new students to be capable of this kind of work, and of course we weren't either at the beginning. In the early years, many were only coming for the loaves and fishes. We all were at the beginning.

We have passed that era now. We are workers in the field. Everyone in this room is ready and accepts that. We are workers in the field and depending on our own spiritual integrity, will we surrender the grasp that human consciousness has on us and really give ourselves up to this high calling. There is nothing glamorous about it; it requires the utmost patience, longsuffering, sacrifice of time, effort, money. We don't have time to cry the blues and don't have time even to spend on our elation when the principle is proven. The main purpose of our work is not to go out and save the world, but to evolve into the Christ-consciousness, the fourth-dimensional consciousness. Our work is not to patch up humanhood. Our work is not to make sick people well or poor people wealthy. That is not our work. The Infinite Way movement has grown so not much healing work needs to be done among Infinite Way students anymore. And the public at large now has the advantage of great strides in the medical profession to handle their ills. Our work is to evolve within ourselves individually and as groups all over the world so that the spiritual influence we carry with us, knowledge that "I and the Father are one and all that the Father hath is mine" and all that I have is yours, that influence, that blessing we carry with us as individuals and groups, goes out into the world and eventually brings the Christ-consciousness to the world.

The kingdom of God is within each individual and it takes only one individual to begin a group activity. In 1962, Joel said after a trip to South Africa, that he had discovered on his visit there were more Infinite Way groups in South Africa than in the United States. That was in 1962. Now you can imagine over the years how that number has lessened. We have been amazed as a group to discover the interest in the work of a group of this nature. All these years we were just working on our own, evolving and coming into the fulness of our mission: service to God through service to humankind. We were just doing our own thing so it never entered our minds that we could be an example. Yet it has gone before us and I would like very much to share my experience of twenty-five years with anyone who would like to start a group; I would be very happy to commit myself to this work.

So for this weekend, our classes will consist of ways and means we have attained to in this group consciousness and hopefully the workshops we have tomorrow afternoon will give you an idea of how that part of our work has expanded;

the students are participating now. They are no longer sitting like little birds waiting to be fed. On Wednesday nights, in rotation, each student is giving a fifteen-minute to twenty-minute class to the group. This has been a terrifying experience for most of them, but you see it is so easy for a student who is sitting, listening to somebody, and drinking it all in, it is so easy just to sit back and relax and let the teacher do the work. We are inclined to think "Well that is easy for teachers because they have all this experience." Every teacher had to start and so these students are being given the opportunity to begin in the bosom of friends, protected by love and encouraged by spiritual support so that when their time comes, they will have a familiarity with opening out a way for the imprisoned splendor to escape. I feel this is the blessing and I think they do too once they get over the initial shock of getting up to speak.

Then, once a month we have the practitioners' workshop. They too rotate and in turn lead a workshop. Some of them are wonderful, some of them are hilarious; in other words, we are permitting spiritual spontaneity to escape. And then once a month we have the business and professional workshop; if you have heard any of the recordings, you know what they are doing. As each one gives a workshop, you can feel the consciousness growing and deepening. You can feel the spiritual confidence coming through, the conviction which is the Spirit. You can't trust the principle until you see it proven, but when you see it proven, you have the conviction and then the Spirit comes through. That to me is what the Spirit is. When I speak to you, I speak with conviction, with Spirit, because I have seen these principles proven over and over and over in ways I could never have outlined.

Proving the Principles

My own personal experiences in proving the principles came through experiences of healing. I have found that the healing work deepens your consciousness because each healing is different than the time before. There is no formula. Something different comes through and there have been some tremendous experiences in healing work that I have had which I would like to share with you.

The very first healing that ever came to me happened before I got into The Infinite Way and I feel it was responsible for bringing me into The Infinite Way. My little son who was only seven weeks old had been born with chronic bronchial asthma, and he was having great difficulty breathing. My husband and I took him to a pediatrician who diagnosed it and put him on medication which didn't help at all. My husband who was frightened thought we should go to another pediatrician who in a very funereal tone told us that the child couldn't possibly live longer than six months with a disease like that. Well, that angered my husband and upset me, and we picked the child up and took him home.

That night the baby was laboring so. I was in his nursery and sitting on a chair with the little night light on and he was in his crib. We had done everything we could; we had used medication, steam, everything we knew to do. My husband was asleep, and as I sat there, first in fear, then utter helplessness, I grew quiet. It was just like I gave up; there was nothing else I could do. And in the darkness the voice spoke and said, "Before he was thine, he was mine." At that, I completely relaxed and in minutes the child was breathing freely. That healing has continued to this day and at thirty-four years old, he is a beautiful unfolding spirit, who incidentally has never asked or has needed to be taught.

Now it was about a year and a half later when *Practicing the Presence* came into my hand. At that time Joel was taking The Infinite Way student body into mysticism and evidently my consciousness was ready for mysticism even though I'd had no metaphysics whatsoever. Within a few months I had calls. My first call for healing work was kidney cancer. I didn't know what to do. I was terrified. I turned from the phone and asked, "What do I do?" I walked into the living room and sat down and went into meditation and felt this tremendous billowing pouring of Love as a substance, a spiritual substance. This woman was to go into surgery the following morning, and about one o'clock that afternoon the following day she called me, and I said, "You are out of surgery?" She replied, "Oh they decided to give me another test this morning, and they decided it didn't need surgery." So that was the first healing. The second one, about two weeks later, was a terminal claim of lupus. My mother called, very emotional and very upset, and told me my sister was dying of lupus. Once again—and I was emotional, this was my sister—I wasn't spiritual, I wasn't indifferent, I sat down and wondered what to do. Once again, I had this same experience, this billowing experience. By nightfall my sister, too, had had what they call a recession of the disease and she lived another eighteen years.

These were my first experiences with healing, but then I had to go back and learn the metaphysics because Joel said if I was ever to teach, I would have to be able to distinguish between other metaphysical teachings and The Infinite Way. The work always begins with one. And by the end of my first year of study, under Joel's direction, I took a small group of students from Unity, and that is how I began. Knowing very little but going into it with all my heart and soul—that is the beginning of pouring—the surrender to the Spirit, to the healing work, the teaching work, the educational part of it, the spiritual part of it; *I* performing that which is appointed for you. And a spiritual work is certainly appointed for each and every one of you regardless of who you are and what you think is your mundane world. Bloom where you are planted.

Tomorrow we will take up some disciplines. Thank you very much. Can we have a closing meditation?

Dominion Through the Disciplines

A Teacher's Responsibility

GOOD MORNING. The reason there are so few dedicated groups in The Infinite Way is because there are too few dedicated teachers. When we take on or say "yes" to the challenge of a group activity, we assume a sacred and grave responsibility for the unfolding spiritual faculties of the souls of those students who come to us. This requires a dedication beyond what we know humanly. It involves an almost constant rehearsal of disciplines and principles in our mind. The first thing we do with students is to give instructions on the spiritual principles, pour them into their minds, for the purpose of spiritualizing the mind which has formerly been filled with erroneous concepts, erroneous beliefs, based on the belief of good and evil or what is called the mortal or carnal mind.

In order to transform that mind, we have been given these disciplines which have to be practiced constantly, which have to be rehearsed and applied on a daily basis as frequently as they come to your mind or as frequently as you can bring them to your mind. There are students who set timers, and some of mine have done that over the years, to remind them every fifteen minutes or every half-hour or every hour to bring the principles or the disciplines to mind and set them like concrete into the substance which is mind.

Now, in order to qualify as a group leader, there are some aspects of the Christ-consciousness that must be present at the outset. One of them is a thorough knowledge of The Infinite Way writings and Joel's classwork. Another, of course, a dedication to The Infinite Way principles and the goal of illumination. Now I doubt that there is anyone who started as a leader of a tape group or a small activity who has attained full illumination. I don't know of anyone on earth who has attained the fullness of illumination, but that is our goal, that is our number one priority. And the students who come to us are seeking that illumination. Now it must be explained to students that a teacher cannot take a student into the kingdom of heaven. This is a misconception that I have seen down through the years with many Infinite Way students.

A teacher is a way-shower. A teacher is a pointer to the way. A teacher shows, by demonstration, the way. And whatever light the teacher has, manifests, just as all of spiritual consciousness manifests. So that is what the student is coming for, that little bit of light. As you, the teacher, pour, and as you discipline yourself to discern the Christhood of the student, your understanding of the fourth-dimensional consciousness expands. As ye teach, ye are taught.

Last night I said I didn't have much when I started, and I didn't. What I started with was this: In my first spiritual experience, after I came under Joel's consciousness, I had a very deep all-encompassing awareness of the Presence. One day the voice spoke, and said, "This is your way, walk ye in it." That was my basis of understanding: an experience of a Presence that was greater than me. Eventually I learned through the healing work that this Presence was with me always and it performed that which was appointed for me to do. What is appointed for us to do is never a mundane task.

What is appointed for us to do is a spiritual responsibility for which that Presence within goes before us to prepare the way and stays behind us as a blessing. As I grew spiritually and attracted some students to me, there came an awesome feeling of responsibility. Nobody will ever feel adequate to lead or teach. Nobody is in danger of becoming ego driven if they are touched by the Spirit of God.

It is a most humbling experience to be asked to share your light and realize what a small distance you have come and how far you have to go. But if you are spiritually courageous and spiritually wise, you will say yes, because this is your initiation into Christhood. If ever anyone approaches you and asks you for help, and you say no, you have closed the door to the fourth-dimensional consciousness and you are back in humanhood. In my unfoldment on group illumination, it also came to me that the spiritually courageous will inherit the kingdom of God and the spiritually meek will inherit the earth. Now we know what the earth is. We have been here so many lifetimes it is an old familiar place.

Some of us are what are called "old souls." It is sort of like planning to go on a trip and knowing what it is going to be like before you get there and you lose all desire to go. That is the way I feel about humanhood. I have been here so many times I really don't care about it. It does not matter to me what goes on in humanhood; it cannot tempt me. But I didn't arrive at that until after years of being an instrument through which students pulled what they needed for their own spiritual unfoldment.

In taking on a group activity, and it makes no difference if it is two or three or two hundred or three thousand, if it is your flock there is only one and I am that one. Numbers make no difference. It is the quality of the work that pours through the consciousness of you as a leader that matters, and the quality of the consciousness of the students you draw to yourself. Some are more difficult to break through to than others, but you will never be asked to lead or to teach or be given the opportunity to lead or to teach, until some measure of the Christ-consciousness is evident to those who come to you.

That is the recognition of your Christhood, seemingly from outside yourself. But what is really happening is the reflection back to you of your inner conviction of your own Christ. Oneness is the basic principle of any spiritual teaching. There are only three spiritual principles and they are: omnipresence, omnipotence, and omniscience. Every other facet of the spiritual teaching that we call a principle is really just an aspect or a facet of those three principles.

A Teacher's Discipline

In leading and guiding students, we have to bring them to a state of self-discipline. In order to do that, we ourselves have to be disciplined. It was to this end, Joel gave us the way to do that. To impart the disciplines to your students, you explain to them that they have to have the willingness and the openness to practice. You cannot teach anyone who is not open and receptive to your own state of consciousness. And bear in mind, too, the students in a group cannot rise any higher than the leader's state of consciousness. That is why it is imperative that leaders remain in their sacred duty to their students and remain in the highest state of spiritual consciousness possible. You can't do it 100 percent of the time, but it is up to you in your self-discipline to discern when you are being drawn into humanhood and when you need to stand back and pull yourself up out of the muck and mire; if not, you'll be the blind leading the blind.

Now nobody likes to hear about the disciplines. That is because humanly we are often in a state of inertia and we love to justify a lack of self-discipline by saying "Oh that impinges on my freedom." Well, let me tell you, in humanhood you don't have any freedom. You are held in bondage, in slavery, to a totally false, erroneous, and illusory world. Freedom is the breaking out of that. Freedom comes with assuming dominion over that mind you've let govern your lives, over that body you let tell you what to do and how to eat, when to go to sleep, or when to get sick. In assuming this dominion, we begin a program of around-the-clock discipline. Now I know that all of you know these disciplines, but I will repeat them here as a part of your training in assuming leadership of groups. This has to be imparted to your students, but you cannot teach anything you cannot prove. If you are not doing this, they will know it; you will be uncertain, and they will know that too. You can't fool the students and the students can't fool the teacher. The teacher can look right into the mind and the soul of the students. Well, unbeknownst to them, the student can also make that same discernment of the teacher.

In the morning then, upon awakening, the very first thing, before our feet touch the floor, we close our eyes and go within and make our contact. We inquire sometimes, "What have you to do for me today?" or "What have I in the house?" as we said last night. Or, we remember that, "This is the day the Lord has made" and "I and the Father are one." And "Lead me and guide me in thy name, in thy righteousness," depending on your own nature, whether it is devout, whether it is pious, whether it is a go-getter, whether it is metaphysically inclined, or whether it is totally surrendered. There is no formula to this type of thing; it depends on you and you will find your own rhythm. Having done that and made your contact, then you are free to get up and go about your business.

Before you leave the house, you make this contact again, with the realization that "Thou goest before me to prepareth the way, and Thou stays behind me as a blessing." Now this "Thou" we are talking about is not a person. There is no God up in the sky to go before you to protect you and prepare your way and there is no God who is going to stay behind you because you are so special, to bless your household and your neighborhood. That "Thou" we are talking about is your very own consciousness, your very own grasp or understanding of these spiritual principles and disciplines. That "Thou" you are leaving behind as a blessing is your awareness that your consciousness is there in your home and in your community or rather, that home and that community is in your consciousness. And therefore, it *is* you because you are a state of spiritual consciousness. That is the blessing you leave behind: your awareness of this truth that where I am, God is, and that is the blessing. The Presence that goes before you to make the crooked places straight is your consciousness. Where then are you going? Are you going to a job that you hate to go to? Are you going to school to be educated in a subject you don't care about? Or are you going as a blessing to the world? That is the consciousness that goes before you; that is the Presence that goes before you.

Some of you here are teachers in elementary school and high school. If you don't make this law for yourself before you leave home, you are not going to be a blessing to your students. You are going to see them as rowdy and hopeless most of the time. Once in a while there will be events of something shining in them but that will be accidental, unless the law has been made in your consciousness: knowing *I* have dominion over this day and that "He performeth that which is appointed for me" and that "He" is my awareness of spiritual law and *I* am assuming dominion over my world which is a reflection of my consciousness.

Now, as you are schooled in that discipline you will not only lead human beings, you will attract those to you to be led spiritually. This is a way of life. When the voice spoke to me and said, "This is your way, walk ye in it," that meant the dedicated Christ. Over the years there have been times, not only for me, but I have heard other leaders and teachers say this, there are times when you feel fraudulent. There are times when you feel you just want to stick your head in the sand and cry. "What in the world am I doing assuming leadership of these students? I know nothing. I am the blind leading the blind." But in those moments of an incredible sense of worthlessness, a light comes, and you realize that that is just one more way of emptying out, of destroying the human sense of ego.

In our belief that we are something of ourselves we are held in human consciousness. We want to accomplish. This is why we don't of our own selves set out to form a spiritual group activity. The only way we know we are ready is when someone asks. Or if we see this interest, this little bud in an acquaintance's consciousness and we feel led of the Spirit to invite them to share a recording or to lend them a book. This is perfectly permissible. But to try to impose your spiritual conviction on others before they are ready for it will only cause you to lose it. And you know why? Because you are seeing two. You are seeing someone in need of God instead of seeing God itself appearing before you. There is only one I; we all call ourselves by the name of God, I. It is just multiplied form.

So, as students come to you and you say yes to this challenge, you are consciously committed to sharing with these students or these friends and you have to remember that everything you share, you are sharing with yourself. The minute you have two, you are losing it. It is the same with any form of supply. If you pay a bill and you think you are paying somebody for services rendered or if you give to your spiritual activity and you feel that you are paying a leader for services rendered, you are losing it. You are losing it. That can never come back to you because you have two. You are giving something to somebody else and you feel you are depleted by doing so.

"Let's Change Our Minds"

In the spiritual activity, as I speak to you, I am speaking to myself. I am speaking out of this wisdom and experience of my spiritual consciousness which has been developed over these last thirty-two years and heaven knows how many lifetimes before that through the practice of these disciplines. In order to spiritualize our mind, we have to keep it filled with truth. In *The Infinite Way* book, Joel says "a mind imbued with spiritual truth, is a law unto your experience." Now your experience in your world belongs to nobody else, it is yours. It has no dominion over you; the creature cannot talk back to the creator. Each of us has to accept the responsibility that we have created our own world. If we don't like it, then we have to have a change of consciousness, and the way we change that consciousness is to change our minds.

We had a wonderful experience with that in the business class by using that phrase. "Let's change our minds." It is in changing your minds that your world changes because your world is reflected back to you through the instrument of the mind. Years ago, the first principle that I worked on and had some insight into was omnipotence. "Two powers" was very strong in my human awareness. Then, with the aid of *The Thunder of Silence*,* which incidentally, Joel told me not to read—but then I had to read it [laughter]—I really came into a spiritual clarification of "no-power." In the course of discerning that, the instrument of the mind began to unfold a little to me. Most human beings think the mind is like the brain, that it is a physical function. So, I began to do a lot of work on the mind. I was, really, not curious. I was almost in despair to find out what the mind is, because I knew it wasn't in my body.

One day I was meditating on the mind and about to give up when the voice spoke and said, "You are looking at it." Suddenly I understood; the mind is the mirror. We think this is a world out here, we think this is real, we think this is compact, this is physical, and I saw clearly that these are nothing but images and *this* is my mind. And this mind contains my consciousness of life. It contains my consciousness of friendship, of companionship, of supply, it contains my consciousness, period. Everything I hold in my consciousness is manifested in my mind and reflected back to me. And in the case of a flawed consciousness, it is reflected back to me in a magnified state so I'll be sure not to miss it.

So, if you are misbehaving in a terrible manner to me, I have no one to blame but myself. This is a challenge to me: either to see through the appearance to the reality, or to drop the concept which I am imposing on your countenance. That is why nobody out there has any power over you. We cannot get off the ground until we begin to practice the disciplines, to spiritualize mind so that our reflections begin to stare at us from a different base.

---

* Joel S. Goldsmith, *The Thunder of Silence* (Longboat Key, FL : Acropolis Books).

I look out at you this morning and what do I see? Beautiful students on the path to the fourth-dimensional consciousness. I see students ready to enter the third degree of Christhood. I see friends and companions. I see family. This is my family. Now, what does that say about my consciousness? And what does it say about your consciousness? Because I'm sure you are seeing in each other the same thing. See how far you have come? Now the trick is, when you leave this room, and encounter who knows what appearances, to see the same thing.

The Student's Work

Your world, and it cannot be emphasized too much, is an out-picturing of your own consciousness. If you are in human consciousness, it will be reflected back to you in infinite false concepts. When you discover, as I'm sure you already have—and which you will have to teach to the students who come to you—that you don't like what you are looking at, you don't like your world, then it becomes your God-given responsibility and dominion to change your world. God cannot give us dominion. We already have it. It is the exercise of it that we are lazy about. We come into a spiritual teaching under the umbrella of a teacher's consciousness with the false assumption that that consciousness is suddenly going to become ours, without making any effort for it. There are students who will ask you for spiritual healing and will hang up the telephone and go shopping or go to the movies. "I've dropped it so let the practitioner handle it." That is not the way students should be taught except in the case of patients outside The Infinite Way who are rarer and rarer because of the improvement in the medical profession and the technologies they have come up with.

But it should be explained in your leadership that it is equally important for the student to work as it is for the practitioner to work. Don't ever let somebody who says they want to progress on the spiritual path come to you and dump problems at your doorstep and walk off to play tennis. This is completely wrong. The students must be taught that their responsibility is equal to yours or should be. You have every right to expect the same integrity, the same honesty, and the same loyalty from the students who come to you as they expect of you.

This is a one-way street. It is very difficult not to see the humanhood of the people around you. But as in the example I gave you last night of my husband saying "I will take care of that," take the time to listen. We are so busy trying to interrupt people. I know people who are married who finish each other's sentences. In watching them I wonder what kind of communication is this? Neither one is talking about the same thing, yet they assume they are. Have you ever been on the telephone talking to somebody and somebody behind you is talking to that person over your shoulder forming a concept or putting words in your mouth to say? That kind of thing should never be permitted. You should never accept a suggestion from anyone about anything serious or important in your life. Find out for yourself. Go within. Receive your own inner guidance. And while not accepting suggestions from other people, we free ourselves from giving suggestions. That too is erroneous.

The only thing we are permitted in our work is to share spiritual principles and to drop all judgments, even about whether the students practice or not. If they don't practice, sooner or later, they will either drop away or you will have to say to them "I'm sorry I don't think I have anything for you." But from the outset, you have to condition yourself to be a disciplinarian and to be able prove what you teach. It's never "don't do as I do, do as I say." Never that. It is "do as I do, and you may possibly be where I am."

Once you establish the disciplines in the student's consciousness, then you can begin to work with the principles. Joel has a list of chapters he was very strong that we practice and which he taught us to require students who came to us, not just read, but work with. They are: "The New Horizon" in *The Infinite Way*; "God is One" in *Living the Infinite Way*; "Protection" in *The 1955 Infinite Way Letters;* "Break the Fetters that Bind You" in *The 1958 Infinite Way Letters*; "Contemplation Develops the Beholder" in *The Contemplative Life*; "Introduction" and "Love Thy Neighbor" in *Practicing the Presence*; and "The Relationship of Oneness" in *The Art of Spiritual Healing*. These chapters encompass the principles of The Infinite Way and any one of these principles, if grasped, will make it easier for the student to grasp and to practice the others.[*]

I found in my unfoldment on omnipotence that it was then easy to go to omnipresence. There was another student who was very close to me, who found omnipresence easier to grasp. We were both students of Joel and were very close friends, 2000 miles apart, but we corresponded and talked on the telephone. All we ever discussed though were principles; we didn't share our inner experiences or our letters from

---

[*] Joel S. Goldsmith, *The Infinite Way* (Camarillo, CA : DeVorss & Co.);
Living the Infinite Way (Longboat Key, FL : Acropolis Books, Inc.);
The 1955 Infinite Way Letters and *The 1958 Infinite Way Letters* now published as seperate volumes in *The Heart of Mysticism* series (Longboat Key, FL : Acropolis Books, Inc.);
The Contemplative Life (Longboat Key, FL : Acropolis Books, Inc.);
Practicing the Presence (Longboat Key, FL : Acropolis Books, Inc.);
The Art of Spiritual Healing (Longboat Key, FL : Acropolis Books, Inc.);

Joel. That is another thing that has been encouraged in the student teacher relationship: It is a very sacred experience. Humanly, students will try to gain favor with the teacher and will sometimes let the human concept of competitiveness enter their consciousness when they are seemingly sharing a spiritual experience. But they have to be taught: "Why do you want to share that experience?" They have to be brought to an understanding of why they want to share a sacred experience that has not yet demonstrated itself. Once it is demonstrated you can share it with those whom you are helping. Or even in classwork like this, we share experiences; but if your ego is abroad, it wants to show and tell. You are casting your pearls before swine and the swine is usually your own ego and you lose it.

During my early student days, every time I had this urge to say something to my friend about an experience I had I would ask myself, "Why do I want to tell her that?" Well the appearance was, "I want to share this with my close friend, we are both on the path." That wasn't it. And if you are honest with yourself you know it isn't that. Any experience you have on the inner plane is sacred. That is between you and God or you and the Christ or the fourth-dimensional consciousness—whatever you want to call it—but it is not of this world. So, the minute you try to bring it into this world, you are scattering it before the swine who are right there waiting to gobble it up.

Every time we receive a little bit of light, the world is standing out there just waiting to snatch that light. The world hates truth and those people who are called "good human beings" are the hardest to bring into it. Saintliness is a curse; I know because I have dealt with a couple saints in this group and they are the most difficult to work with.

Sharing Our Spiritual Supply

So there are multitudinous facets of any student's consciousness when they come to you to be enlightened and it is very disturbing when we feel we have so little to share but here we come again to spiritual supply. Nothing you are ever going to know with your intellect, nothing you are ever going to know with your mind and your human education is going to prepare you for this work. It is what you draw forth in a transcendental experience, and by transcendental experience, we mean transcending this that you can taste, hear, touch, see and smell: the mind, the human mind. We transcend this appearance and the word of God flows through our awareness and the presence of God makes itself known and we are conscious of that. And whatever we are conscious of then flows into the mind and impresses itself and reflects back to us. That is where it comes from; it never comes from out here. Supply, remember, is outgo, not income.

In *The Contemplative Life,* in the chapter "Supply and Secrecy," Joel says: "Supply is just as spiritual as integrity, loyalty, morality, and honesty." But we cannot pray for these qualities because they are already embodied in our consciousness, whether or not we are experiencing them or expressing them to the fullest of our understanding. Who doubts that we possess a full measure of integrity, honesty, loyalty, fidelity, and benevolence? The question is, to what extent do we wish to express it? Or what excuses do we make for leaving them unexpressed?

As human beings we are full of justifications about why we do not give here and why we do not give there, why we hold on, why we withhold. You remember Ananias and Sapphira withheld from the Christ and you know what happened to them. What happens to us when, once knowing this principle, we withhold the expression of it? We drop dead; we fall right back into humanhood, which is the muck and mire of all existence. We cannot withhold, we cannot think that this belongs to me. All that we are, God is. We have inherited all that the Father has and it does not belong to us. We are transfer agents through which not only the beautiful spiritual qualities flow to the students who come to us, but also the monetary things, the forms that we use.

Many people who complain about a lack of supply when they mean a lack of money don't even clean their clothes closets out. They wouldn't share a crust of bread with the birds and they wonder why they lack supply. Never, never, should we store up material things where moth and rust corrupt. Always we should believe that we are the funnel through which all things flow—all things. Whatever the need is, *I* am the very incarnation of love. What does love do? It meets the need. Whether it is healing, whether it is a cup of water, whether it is a friendly hand, or a piece of clothing, or if it is a beggar appearing at the door.

This was my early training in the Depression. In those days there were whole families walking along the rural areas on highways, when people were literally in the streets, literally homeless, not by choice, and not because of drugs or mental illness. It was a pitiful sight. We didn't have much. My father was fortunate enough to have a job as a long-distance truck driver. I remember he made thirty dollars a week when I was a child and we thought we were so blessed and fortunate. We lived in the country where there was a highway in front and these small families used to come by regularly. The father would be carrying a child and the mother would be carrying a baby, mostly shoeless, cold, hungry, and my mother would bring them into our house which was isolated but still on the highway and share our food. I learned by watching her. She never instructed me verbally; she showed me how to serve God through serving humankind from her point of view. And in return, I also observed this: the men would always ask what they could do for her before they moved on. Could they chop some wood for her? Could they sweep the yard for her in order to maintain their dignity and to make the sharing come full circle? This I observed as a child and it stuck with me.

Supply is as spiritual as any other spiritual quality that we call intangible. And to experience it, it must be expressed by us, not expressed to us, expressed through us. Supply is not something that comes to us; it is something that goes out from us and then returns. The bread that we cast upon the waters is the only bread possible to come back to us. The reason there are so many people with burnt fingers is because they are trying to get somebody else's bread away from them and you know that is not possible. You can steal from somebody and that individual will still get their own and you will lose yours.

Life does not permit us to take from others what belongs to them and therefore the only supply to which we have spiritual title is the bread that we ourselves place on the waters of life. What goes out from us is exactly what comes back to us pressed down and running over. But it cannot come back to us unless we first send it out.

Now this is spiritual law. Sometimes we say "Well I'm working so hard and I know I'm so well qualified in my job but I'm not being paid enough, nobody's appreciating me." Or "I'm worth more money." When I hear that I ask "Well what did hinder you? Who's setting this value on you? Who are you letting set this value on you?" We have dominion; we don't accept anyone else's estimate of our worth. We know our worth and when we accept someone else's estimate of it what are we doing? We are giving up our dominion. Now another person might not ever agree with you on your monetary worth or your moral worth or your spiritual worth. That's beside the point. You are not dependent on anyone. The only thing you are dependent on is your own consciousness and that includes your realization of your worth. That's not being cantankerous or disagreeable, that's assuming dominion.

I remember a student telling a story not long ago. She had reached a certain level in her business activity, and she felt that she was worth more money. So she went to her employer and said that she would like to be raised to a salary rate that was appropriate for the job that she was doing. Her employer came back with a suggested increase and she said, "No I cannot accept that," and she reiterated: "I'm asking for a salary that is appropriate for the job that I am doing." A day or so later she met her boss in the hall and they chatted a second. By then, she had decided, "Well, if they don't come through, then I'll find a place where I'll receive the appropriate compensation for my worth." This boss spoke to her and said that something was going to be done and when they came back with another offer it was appropriate and they had an agreement.

There are other students who say "I've reached the top of my salary line, this is as far as I can go." Well now I ask you "Who told you that was the top of your salary line? Who told you that?" At some time or another somebody had to set that and before they set that top salary there was another top salary beneath it. Human rules and human laws always need to be broken. Only that which comes of God is permanent.

Before we close I would like to add this. There is a rumor that I heard recently that The Infinite Way is dead. Now you know to me that is hysterical because The Infinite Way is an emanation of pure Spirit. I mean that would be like saying Christianity is dead or Buddhism is dead. These are spiritual principles emanating from the Source itself and being interpreted by us in a way that we can understand.

Now our interpretation might die. But the principles of The Infinite Way cannot die because what God has joined together no one can put asunder. Further, you and I *are* The Infinite Way consciousness. So you can see how ridiculous a statement like that is. A spiritual teaching will grow and expand and meet the needs of each generation in each age. That is why we are sitting here today because this is another phase of The Infinite Way activity, hopefully an expansion of our work here and a new plateau for incoming students. I know that the generation below me needs a different terminology. They have different needs which have to be met. But the difficulty is in holding succeeding generations to the same principles, the same disciplines, that we have been taught. You cannot rise higher than the principles and you should really understand that.

I think that is all the time we have so thank you very much.

APRIL 1994 HOTEL TALKS

Questions and Answers

IT IS VERY DIFFICULT to begin again after that wonderful performance by the four workshop leaders,* and once again, what a beautiful demonstration of the oneness in consciousness. Students have come to join us here this weekend from other states, and upon their arrival it was as if the entire student body just merged into one Spirit with one goal—illumination. You cannot tell where one begins and one leaves off. It is just a continuous flow of Spirit. For this I thank you! I am very grateful. We will go now to the questions that were submitted.

Q: *Two friends asked about meditation. I suggested they read* The Art of Meditation.** *I don't know if either one bought the book. Was I wrong making this suggestion? Should I have invited them to meditate together instead?*

A: If, in the course of conversation, people ask you if you know anything about meditation, there is certainly no harm

---

* In this class, the participants divided into four groups and each group leader led a workshop with a specific topic. At the end of the day, each workshop leader gave a presentation summarizing their group's experience. See examples in "Contributions."

** Joel S. Goldsmith, *The Art of Meditation* (Longboat Key, FL : Acropolis Books, Inc.)

in revealing that you not only know something about it, but that you practice it, in which case, if they ask to be taught then of course you are willing to help them attain an understanding of meditation. You also must feel perfectly free to suggest any of Joel's books for they all contain something on the art of meditation. But the book *The Art of Meditation* is absolutely proper.

We have come through almost forty-five years of The Infinite Way consciousness flowing into human consciousness, The Infinite Way principles being put into human consciousness. In the beginning, we were very wise to stay under cover and do our work in secret, because, when I came into The Infinite Way, none of the students of my generation even understood the word "consciousness." We had to contemplate what consciousness meant. We meditated long and hard asking, "What is consciousness?" When Joel said to us we were a state of consciousness, we couldn't relate to that, because that understanding takes a few years. I remember Daisy Shigamura* telling me that she had meditated for ten years on the word "consciousness." I am very grateful to Daisy for doing that because I think I gained an understanding in about a year, maybe two. Also, when Joel talked about spiritual principles, I didn't know what he meant. I didn't know what a spiritual principle was. We used to bandy clichés around thinking we knew what we were talking about. We didn't know anything. And so, we did our work in silence and secrecy keeping everything we gleaned from the within to share only with our teacher.

As I said yesterday, my best friend and I did not share any inner experiences, and that was because Joel impressed upon

---

* Daisy Shigamura was one of Joel Goldsmith's early students.

us they must be demonstrated before you can share them, otherwise you lose them. When someone sees something in you and comes to you and asks, then you can share, but share a little bit at a time. You use the term "give a cup of cold water," then as they become more serious and you begin to share a little more with them, they will go deeper and through meditation you begin to lift them.

Traditionally in The Infinite Way, we still take that stance of total secrecy. Yet think how frequently you hear the word consciousness today. It is in almost every paragraph in the newspaper; you hear it on television and it is in fiction. Young people use it all the time. In short, we know on the human scene that consciousness means awareness. So of course it is all right to share things like that. Consider how often you hear and see the word meditation? And contemplation? Even the orthodox churches are using the word meditation. I have friends in the orthodox church who go on retreats and silent meditations all weekend. Now whether they attain anything or not I do not know but they come back refreshed and I am sure they gain something from it. So if they ever asked me "Would you teach me your technique of meditation?" I would be very happy to do so.

We cannot hold on to the old tradition; The Infinite Way is an *infinite* way. Joel never meant for us to be stilted and for us to stagnate in old procedures. The principles never change, and we do not deviate from them. We do not mix The Infinite Way principles with the principles from any other teaching. That would be very confusing, and you would mislead any students who come to you if you do not require that they keep their nose to the grindstone. The students who have come to me over the years know that that is the way I have taught. Nothing else. Put all the other books away. You will either practice these principles or I cannot teach you.

Now after a length of time, when The Infinite Way principles are established in the consciousness of students and they become what we call advanced, then of course they will want to read other books to see the oneness functioning in these other spiritual teachings. While some followers of a teaching may say their teaching is the only one, as you grow in spiritual awareness you discover that all the major teachings on earth are saying the same thing. They are saying one God. And as Joel pointed out on a talk I listened to not long ago, if we would just go into the churches and say "Well I'm talking about your God; there is only one God, and what I have to say about my God I'm saying about your God," then the barriers would be down. So far though, we haven't been invited to do that. Eventually this is what hopefully will come about, that the barriers will be down, and we will be able to share universally the one God of our teaching and bring it into human awareness as the word of God made flesh as you and me. Can you not see that this is the word of God made flesh, the Spirit of God made flesh, in this group this weekend? There is nothing but one Spirit here. One God. That is the word of God made flesh. First appearing individually and now we see it as a group. Is that not evolving consciousness?

Finally, I do not think it would be advisable to say to somebody who is interested in meditation "Well, I'm glad to meditate with you." You see there we are assuming a superior state of consciousness again. That way, all we do is set up a barrier. Wait until the time is right and you have an opening and someone asks, "Will you meditate with me?" This is a basic practice in our Infinite Way work which I think is wisdom. You save yourself a lot of malpractice that way.

Q: *What is the best way to deal with someone who is argumentative? Is it better to deal with them privately or in front of the group?*

A: I assume that this student is asking about someone who is argumentative within the group itself. I feel when confronted with argument or antagonism of any kind, to "agree with thine adversary." I don't respond. If I am speaking and someone interrupts me, I just stay quiet. I stop speaking until they have said what they want to say. In a group context however, if you are leading the group or teaching the group, under no circumstances must you permit discussion or argument in a group activity. The leader has the floor and the flow, and the students who are participating in that group activity must be given our respect because their turn might be next to lead. A participant will get back exactly what he or she has put out. So any leader should be aware of that and if they feel a reaction to the individual who is disturbing the harmony of the group, then they should say, "Can we meditate for a minute." People who meditate together very rarely argue. There is an underlying bond of oneness that is established among people who meditate regularly together. Now in a teacher-student situation, it is advisable to take the student away from the group privately—never make an issue of it—and correct the student. But I don't know of any Infinite Way student after this length of time who would consider arguing with the leader or debating anything from the floor. So, this is a principle—"agree with thine adversary"—which I apply in all areas of my life, not only in our spiritual work.

Q: *How often should a new group have tape classes?*

A: That depends entirely on the group and on the group leader because the leader is, at the beginning, the consciousness of the group and the group itself is being formed under the leader's consciousness. And so, any leader receives their instruction from within—it's a feeling—holding it twice a week or holding it once a week and some people just hold it once a month. Now I can share with you my first experience: When I lived in New England and was a young student under Joel, there were five Unity students in Boston who, in an interesting way, found out I was a student of Joel's and called me on the telephone and asked me to help them. Well, I was in no position to help them; I hardly knew anything for myself. I wrote to Joel to tell him what had happened, and he wrote back and said, "Well, you are the only student in New England, and so you have to take this on—they have come to you, they have sought you out." So I arranged to meet them in Boston—I lived in the suburbs—every Sunday afternoon. We maintained that schedule for the remainder of the time I was in Boston. We met once a week and then they would call me for healing work. Being Unity students, they had a difficult time not discussing but I had my strict instructions from Joel, and I have them to this day.

He had sent me a form letter called "Suggestions Regarding Tape Recording Groups,"[*] and in it he outlines, specifically, the conduct of the leader, the classes that would be helpful to start new students with, and then working right on into the middle order, he even states exactly how to invite people, what to tell them their obligation is to a tape group, and when to tell them you have nothing for them, that you cannot do anything for them. He said, "There are those who attend meetings, who find it impossible to maintain the necessary quiet and it is proven helpful to extend no further invitations to them and permit them to work out their own salvation in their own home while our serious students gather and find the expansion of consciousness they so earnestly seek."

---

[*] Recording 557: 1964 "Instructions for Infinite Way Tape Group Leaders." Available for purchase from www.joelgoldsmith.com.

In other words, it was his point of view and most certainly has been mine over the years that you must not permit argumentation or discussion or any kind of dissension into the aura of the Christ you are trying to establish in a group activity. This is not a timid position to be in. You cannot be timid and be a leader. You either are or you are not. And with your commitment when you first take this job on, that has to be settled in your consciousness; your commitment is first. And though you might have to hurt people's feelings, that is part of it. You cannot be a good human being and do this. You cannot be nice. Joel also tells you that:

> It is customary for students who may possibly be interested to hear the tape recordings, and who attend regularly, to contribute financially to the support expenses incidental to establishing and maintaining the tape-recording activity. It is not really that students are contributing to pay for the tapes, since what they are actually doing is contributing to having tapes available that they may hear and study. The tapes will always remain the property of the person who is conducting the work, and those who contribute toward their purchase should feel that they derive a commensurate benefit from the hearing of these tapes and the privilege of studying them. Naturally it is up to each individual to decide how much they wish to contribute, and no one should be asked to contribute more than they feel they would like to.[*]

Now that is a beginning tape group. Many conducting such an activity, among them myself, have initially found it very difficult to ask for any monetary contribution toward the maintaining of the tape group. It was some time before I was even able to put a bowl out. I had my attention called to it in

---

[*] Handout by Joel S. Goldsmith, *Suggestions for Infinite Way Tape Study for Groups and Individuals.* (paraphrased)

no uncertain terms and received a long-distance telephone call from a teacher who called me out. This was a long time after I had worked with the first tape group; I was already into my second and beginning to teach. This teacher said to me that I must remember I was not doing the students a favor by assuming the support of my own spiritual activity, that I was being "lady bountiful" and depriving the students of their demonstration of supply.

Well of course, I felt they couldn't afford it. Can you beat that? If that is not the blind leading the blind! I felt they couldn't afford it. So that really woke me up and I purchased a beautiful Oriental bowl which I use to this day and that was twenty-six years ago.

Q: *The second part of this question is: Should a tape group leader give advice to the members on their problems? And to what extent?*

A: Well, in the beginning, a student uneducated in the spiritual principles seems to automatically think that the practitioner, the leader, or the teacher is a psychologist—or if not a psychologist, an employment agency, or a doctor, even a marriage counselor—oh that's a biggie. "He said, I said, she said, they said." If you are always listening to one side of any story, how on earth can you give advice? Every problem has two sides, and you don't know what the other party's participation in that problem is. You are only hearing one version of it. You do not even know the other person involved so how can you give advice? I see that as another egotistical desire to be self-important. There are times when it is legitimate to advise people on areas where you have had experience. This is what I call "harmless" advice. You can share your experiences with anyone. But never take the attitude, "Well I wouldn't do it that way, if it was me, I'd do it this way."

You can see how far that will get you and the students or the patient. So our job is to not even deal with a person. It is to deal with our own state of consciousness when these claims or problems hit up against us. What we really should say to the spiritual student is, "Let me meditate on this, let's see what comes through your consciousness as a solution." Now that doesn't make us uncommunicative. If somebody says to you, "I need a new dress," you can say, "well gee, Richards is having a sale next week, maybe you'll find something there," that's not what we are talking about. But if someone comes to you with a problem and says "What would you do? What is your advice on this?" be wise. Lorraine Sinkler* said to me years ago, "Margaret, be as wise as a serpent and harmless as a dove." Those are real words of spiritual wisdom.

Remember, you are not in the advice business. You are in the practice of spiritual principles which lifts us above the need of receiving any advice from the outside. That will keep you out of deep trouble.

Q: *If a person is not being healed, what should the practitioner do?*

A: Well that is a little oblique because to answer that I have to know whether the patient is doing their part. If someone calls me for a healing and I don't hear from them in 48 hours, the claim is dropped out of my consciousness. It is each patient's responsibility to keep the practitioner informed as to whether they have received a healing, whether the condition is the same or whether it is worse. However, if a practitioner works with a patient on a claim for a length of time where there is no response in the patient, then it is the practitioner's obligation and responsibility to say to that patient or student,

---

* Lorraine Sinkler served as long-time editor to Joel S. Goldsmith.

"I don't seem to be helping you. May I recommend another practitioner to you?" And that is the extent of that.

Q: *What do you expect the person to do besides going to the mall after asking for help? Should they meditate? Read? Ponder? or all of the above?*

A: Again, it depends on what is happening here with the patient or the student. If you as a student call me for a physical claim, I expect you to be fully aware that this is an illusory claim, that you are hypnotized to thinking you are having pain or this condition and you are asking for spiritual help to break the hypnotism. I'm expecting you to realize that you are asking for spiritual lifting not the healing of a physical pain. But if anyone calls who is not student but a patient, I do not require anything of them. I never say, "Well you ought to read this book or maybe you ought to come to class" or "When I hang up the phone you go meditate too." No. You don't do that because they don't understand what they are asking for and the healing part of our work is always what Joel called "the bait." It brings people to us for whom the disease or the claim itself is the very prod that turns them toward God; it's a blessing in disguise.

So when these individuals come to a spiritual practitioner thinking they are asking for physical healing or whatever the claim is, what they are really asking for is to know God aright. It is up to the practitioners to discern that, and in the practitioners' discernment, they open up a space in the soul of the individual coming to them. If that patient responds, sooner or later they are going to become a student. But those patients and students who continue to call for help with challenges— we call them opportunities for growth—if they continue to call with disease, dissension, unemployment, lack, all of the negativities of human consciousness, and they only want a temporary lifting out of their dilemma, then sooner or later those healings are going to stop, because it is not in the cards that an individual is to live blessed by the consciousness of another individual. And so those patients or students usually fall away or find another practitioner and for a time experience healing until they come to the same stopping point. Nobody, though, can keep an umbrella over another person just to keep them comfortable in the human scene. That is not our work.

So a student of spiritual truth calling for help should realize that they have the same obligation as the practitioner or a teacher. They are calling to be lifted above the illusory nature of this claim to see it clearly as their part in the healing because believe me it is the Christ of the patient that does the healing. It is the practitioner's recognition of the Christ of the student and the patient that does the work. But it is your own Christhood that brings healing. That would make a whole week's work in itself, teaching that one. But any serious student will, when they hang up that phone, go into meditation and be aware, "This is One. I am referring this to the Christ of my own being and now I'm going to be receptive and still and let it happen." See? So no, I would have some words to say to any student who drops their garbage at my feet and takes off to the movies or the mall. That is not teaching and that is not healing.

Q: *How do you know when it is okay to talk and what should you talk about?*

A: Well I think we covered that in the first question and I assume this student means conversational talk, not lecturing or teaching. As a rule, and I'll repeat this from the first question, you don't say anything unless you are asked and your inner discernment tells you when it is all right to say a word about the spiritual path, or share a cup of cold water. But you never lay your soul bare to a stranger or to the curious. The reason our group stayed under cover for over twenty years is because we didn't want to attract the curious. Believe me, in this group activity no student has ever been solicited. They have had to find us by the most circuitous route that you can imagine. In the beginning, one of our first students had a metaphysical bookstore and people who came in to buy Joel's books would sometimes ask if there was an Infinite Way activity in Atlanta. At that time there were two: ours and another one. This individual would give that person the names of both groups never mentioning which group she was a part of. Then their inner guidance would take them to the group that was selected for them from within themselves. Too, this group member never suggested which book that they should buy. She would always refuse if they asked her, "Which book do you recommend?" She would say, "You just look at them and whichever one appeals to you is the one you need for the moment." That's how secretive we were.

We didn't dare take any outer action, yet enough came to us and it took some years before it would be culled out as the nucleus of this group form. We would never turn anybody away. But many would go quickly when they realized they could not talk about it, or discuss it, they could not argue with you about it, they could not say, "Well, this teaching is like that teaching," and that kind of thing because a serious student would not listen to them. There are no discussions in an Infinite Way activity. You can talk to the teacher about the work, you can talk with each other out of class, but when the principles are being presented there is no discussion, because they are not of any man or woman.

So you know it is okay to talk when you know it is okay to talk. And if that sounds like a Zen koan, I'm sorry but that is the way it is.

Q: *How do you start a group when there are no other students that you know about?*

A: Well you'll have a hard time [laughter].

Q: *For instance, when you move to a new place?*

A: Well, if it were me, I'd meditate. "The Father knoweth your need," just as He knew mine in Massachusetts. When that group found me in Massachusetts, I was married to a man who was one hundred percent antagonistic toward The Infinite Way, God, and eventually, me. After I became a student of Joel's, within two or three months I was being roused at four o'clock in the morning to study and meditate before I woke my family and set them off to school and work. This was unthinkable to my husband, that I would leave the marriage bed at four o'clock in the morning to go pray? And read books? My husband was a high executive with a food company in Boston and one day he was having lunch with his two ad executives, one a woman and one a man. The man was a Christian Scientist and the woman was a Unity student. At this meal, they were comparing notes on Christian Science and Unity over the luncheon table and my husband pipes up and says, "Well you are just as crazy as my wife is. She's got hold of somebody called Goldsmith and she is getting up at four o'clock every morning and not getting more than five hours of sleep every night and it's just driving me crazy and I don't know what gets into you people, you are all religious fanatics."

Well the Unity student's ears perked up because they had had a book of Joel's—and bear in mind now, in order to get

Joel's books, we had to ask the publisher or the book department in The Infinite Way—those were the only two places we could get Joel's books. So this woman had come across one of Joel's books via the grapevine and immediately after lunch she goes and telephones her five friends and they were all excited. Here is a student of Joel Goldsmith. Soon they called me (I lived out in the boondocks) and were so thrilled that they found somebody who is a student of Joel's and asked, "Please start a study group, and work with us." So God really does work in mysterious ways. I never had the heart to tell my husband that he started that group [laughter].

You see, you don't have to worry about the formation of a group or finding one if you are in the right place. If you are in meditation, and you are in touch and you are alert, it will come to you, whatever you need for your unfoldment. God does not place an urge within us without the fulfillment of it, you can be convinced of that.

Q: *Does a beginning teacher call the student concerning progress or does she or he always wait for the student to make the overture?*

A: Always the student makes the overture. The teacher is only working with his or her own consciousness. They are the instrument through which the word of God flows as the principles of The Infinite Way or Buddhism or Christianity, or whatever; they are the instrument. A teacher perceives no person but sits within and dwells in the secret and sacred place of the most High, knowing "My own will come to me." Anyone who has ever taught for any length of time knows that there is never a reason to call a student and ask about their progress because the student doesn't have any idea what their progress is. Only the teacher knows and sometimes this is vague to the teacher for a while, but by their fruits you shall know them so never ever do you call a student. As a matter of fact, if you are any teacher at all, you are not going have time because they will be calling you all the time. All the time.

Q: *Where is it best to hold a tape meeting? Should it be in someone's home, a public place or what about changing the location periodically?*

A: When I started my tape group, I did it in the apartment of the woman who had called me and asked that I start a study group, it was the first one in Boston. I did this for two reasons. Number one, the antagonism of my husband made it impossible for me to hold a meeting in my home on the weekend which was the only time they could meet, and two, her apartment was centrally located and I lived in the suburbs which was 25 miles out. That arrangement worked out fine until later, when consciousness had taken over sufficiently, I could hold it in my home, which I did from there on. Later, when I moved to Tampa, I started a meeting through the means of working in a metaphysical bookstore. The store was very large and I took over the managership of it and later the ownership of it and we held our group meetings there while I was in Tampa. I do not think it advisable to change it periodically. Bear in mind, if you are going to be a tape group leader or a study group leader, this is your consciousness of spiritual activity and the symbolic formation it takes is your consciousness, it's what you interpret as a spiritual center or spiritual study group. So if you move the location periodically and it is not necessary, I can't imagine why you would do that unless you were going to go from one person's house to another. I do know a group out in California who meet at each other's homes in rotation.

A working group knows it comes under the consciousness of the leader until the group is developed, such as this one is, and participation begins. You are not going to form a group and have group participation such as we have here any time soon after you form that group and those of you who have been in The Infinite Way for a while know that. It takes years to build that group consciousness of the principles, you see? We are resting here on the basic principle of oneness. You are not going to bring two, three, four, five, fifteen people together from all walks of life and immediately establish an experience of oneness. So until that time comes, the one leading the group is consciously aware of the unfolding unity of that group. It is under the consciousness of that leader and it is always under the consciousness of that leader.

Here let me point something out. If I left today, if I made my transition today, this group would undoubtedly retain their spiritual unity, but it would be different. It would no longer be under my consciousness; the study center is my consciousness of study center, you see. It is theirs too, because they love it and they come, and it is ours. But it was I who formed it. I, from this point of view okay? You with me? So that when you begin a study group, you have to keep that in mind. This is my consciousness functioning from this individual expression and uniquely so. If one of my students opened a study center, I'm sure it would be different from mine. Basically, the arrangement of it might be the same but they would want a different location, a different décor and there would be a different spirit with that leader sitting up there instead of me. The same one Spirit, but uniquely his or her own expression.

So never do you release any of this flow coming through you that is uniquely you, you never scatter that. Remember when I said, don't take suggestions from anybody? And don't make any suggestions to anybody? I don't mean recommendations as, "You might like this book." To suggest something is to try to impose your taste and your will and your likes and dislikes on somebody else. Or even your vision on somebody else. If it is your vision, you do it yourself, you see? You don't manipulate anybody else, and you do not allow anybody to manipulate you. So when you sit in that chair as a leader, you are going to feel something coming down, and it is going to be different from anything you ever felt before. These four people who sat here today during the workshop presentations will tell you that.

It is an experience that elevates you to the position of leadership. Now remember, that is a position of leadership like the presidency of the United States. No person is ever going to foul the office of the presidency of the United States no matter what they do or don't do. That is God ordained. They could only destroy themselves.

The same thing happens in a leadership and teaching capacity. You cannot foul that state of consciousness; you can only fall from grace. But the state of consciousness remains. That's how impersonal it is. You can't bring it down. There are teachers and leaders in high places who do seem to foul the teaching profession or the high office, but they cannot bring it down. All they do is alienate followers. So you have to remember that. When I say this is a grave responsibility that's exactly what I mean. Remember Joel said, "If you can say 'no,' then do so." Do not look for this. Do not let your ego say, "Well I'm ready for a group and so how do I go about getting one?" The group gets you, you don't get the group. You wait until somebody comes or you get an inner instruction.

Now I received an inner instruction to come to Atlanta and I received an inner instruction to start that group in Massachusetts, but in both cases I was approached first. Too, I was invited to come to Atlanta.

Q: *Should an individual who is interested in opening a center have some experience as an Infinite Way teacher or practitioner?*

A: Yes indeed. Starting a study group is a little different from opening a study center. Opening a study center, you become the representative of The Infinite Way teaching. A sign goes on your door.* So you must be in position, if someone walks through that door and says, "Would you help me? Would you do some healing work for me?" you have to be in that consciousness that says, "Yes I can, yes I will," with no hesitation whatsoever. And there is no way you can do that without some conviction that the principles work. You have to have something of a healing consciousness; you have to have had some experience with this that says to you, as one of our workshop leaders said today, "The proof of this stuff is so evident that now I can do it. I know it is true."

We have been proving these principles all of our lives. Not for anybody out here, no, no! Never for the world. For us. For ourselves. And when they are proven in my consciousness, they are proven in your consciousness, because there is but one consciousness and one mind. If I know it, it is known. If you know it, I can know it. And the minute I have a spiritual principle revealed to me or a healing takes place in my consciousness or a revelation takes place in my consciousness, it flows through me into the mind, impresses itself upon the mind and there it is available for all humankind. That's how physicists in Europe and physicists in the United States who never saw each other could come up with the same formula at the same time for great scientific breakthroughs. They have picked up on that spiritual idea.

---

* The sign on the door for this center was The Atlanta Study Center.

Therefore, when we talk about our resources and our Source, and we want to go within to contact that, go within with intelligence. If it is known, I know it. There is a solution to every problem within consciousness. There is no solution out here in the mind. But for every problem that is presented to us, the solution can be found within the realm of the fourth-dimensional consciousness.

Q: *The next question is speaking about the location and various activities appropriate to a study center.*

A: We have copies of our activities out there on the table which you are welcome to take and they list the activities I think are appropriate to study centers. They are many and we keep adding more as the need arises. The location, of course, is very important and you should make it as convenient as possible to find right off an expressway, if you live in a big city, or in a downtown location if most of your students come from that area; in a suburban area such as ours, a good location is close to the expressway, access to downtown and the airport and most of us live out in that area. I'm sorry we have no more time. This has been the grandest experience for me and I hope for you. And I welcome all of you lovely, lovely students who have joined us and merged so beautifully in that spirit of Oneness. Come again and again and again. I love you all. Thank you!

OCTOBER 1994
ATLANTA STUDY CENTER CLASSES

Mind and the Intellect
~Session One~

G OOD MORNING. It is wonderful to see you all again! It seems longer than six months since we all got together. Our subject for this week's work is what I consider very deep, introspective, concentrated work on the mind and the intellect.

The Inner Teacher

There is a story about a woman who once accepted a job as a teacher in an elementary school and upon signing the contract she did not read that she would also be required to handle the music department. Since she knew absolutely nothing about music and could not play an instrument, when she was told by the principal on her first day at school that they were expecting her in the music department, she was aghast. However, being a metaphysical student, she asked them to give her a day to think it over. Of course, her job was at stake if she couldn't handle the music. All night she prayed about this dilemma and when she awakened in the morning, she decided that she would stand on the principle of "Before they call, I will answer," and the other principle, "He performeth that which is appointed for me." That day she went to school, sat down at the piano and suddenly felt as if she were transported into another world and she played the piano beautifully and conducted the music department for two years having never played or read a note of music. Now that is faith, that is conviction, and that is one of the sub-topics we will take up in our work today on the mind, and how the mind works, and the difference between the mind and the intellect.

Now I know that some of you who are with us today have not had the experience of a long-term one-on-one relationship with a teacher of The Infinite Way. Well, it has its advantages and its disadvantages. When you come under the consciousness of a teacher of any spiritual work, it is for the sole purpose of deriving the benefit of that teacher's spiritual consciousness. This is not an academic work, and so in a one-on-one teacher/student relationship the student is privileged, and so is the teacher, to work day in and day out with the spiritual awareness of these principles that have come through and are being demonstrated by the teacher.

The principles, regardless of who is teaching them, always remain the same, but each teacher has his or her own unique expression. So bear in mind this week, that what we are studying and what we are working with is not arguable, it is not debatable. You can disagree with the unfoldment which I assure you I have never heard or read anywhere about the mind and the intellect. That does not mean it is infallible; it does not mean it is the ultimate. It only means that it is my unfoldment over a thirty-three-year period. I'll also tell you those who are new, that the students who have been in this work with me for over twenty years have been given most of this unfoldment two or three times over the years and have not grasped it, so it will be new to them today as well. And of course, it has deepened for me over the years. As I said, this is not the ultimate and it is not infallible; it is my unfolding spiritual consciousness on mind and the intellect. If you disagree with it, that is your privilege, but it is not debatable. There are always other teachers who have not yet had this unfoldment [laughter]. So here we go.

Mind Is a Transparency

We've all studied *The Thunder of Silence*; we have all heard many of Joel's talks on the subject of the mind, and if you will remember, his unfoldment that mind is not God was original and unique and created an explosion in spiritual consciousness. His entire unfoldment is based, of course, on the principles of mind as a transparency and as a non-creative faculty. So let us take up our work from the basis of mind as the infinite instrument of consciousness: Our first principle is: I am consciousness; I am Spirit, and mind is my instrument to reflect back to me that which I am. Now let's just play with our individual awareness of this. Let's not try to take in the universal *I* at this moment. Let's just see how it works with the personal I individually.

It must be thirty-two or thirty-three years since I had my first insight with mind. I had been diligently studying *The Thunder of Silence* and intuitively knew that if I didn't understand what mind is and how it works, I would never be able to do spiritual healing because I recognized it as the instrument through which spiritual healing would flow. In the class in April, I recounted to you several incidents early on in my work where spiritual healing occurred and three so-called terminal diseases were healed without my really being grounded in the letter of truth. Though I came to know this as real spiritual healing, I did not know how it was done. In setting about filling my mind with the principles and the letter of truth, I was following instructions the same as every one of you have done. You have all read and studied the books; you have all listened to the tapes, and I am sure that you are at the place in consciousness where you realize that what you are doing is reconditioning your mind.

Over the years, the terms "mind" and "intellect" have been interchangeable: When someone speaks of the intellect, they think they are speaking of the mind, and when someone speaks of the mind, they think they are speaking of the intellect. We use those two words interchangeably, but they are not the same. My own unfoldment on the intellect came about twenty years ago—and that was another little explosion in consciousness—that the intellect was an adjunct of the mind.

At that time, I was working on what the mind was and was extremely frustrated. Like everyone else, I thought thoughts were of the mind, that my mind controls me, that I had to still my mind in order to meditate, that I had to transcend my mind, and so forth and so on. Then one day, in my frustration, I struck a chord when I asked, "What is the mind?" And the voice came back and said, "You are looking at it!" That was a revelation.

Since that time, day by day, I have been working with this principle that I don't have to transcend my mind, I am transcendent of my mind, because mind fills all space. What we call space is mind, and there is nowhere I can go that my mind is not. When the astronauts went into what was called outer space, what greeted them when they reached the moon but the mind? How could they have known it was the moon if it were not the mind reflecting back their concept of moon, of planets, of stars, of space? Mind fills all space.

This was brought home to me just a few weeks ago. I had my two little grandchildren in the car with me and we headed out to lunch. The youngest one who is five was in the back seat and he said, "Grammy? What is space?" Well, I thought, "What *is* space?" Then I realized this was a wonderful opportunity, so I stopped the car and said, "Let's get out." On the side of the road there was a field, there were trees, and I said, "All of this is space, but you don't know it and you can't see it until you look at the forms. It is the forms that explain to us what this is because space is invisible." Now I didn't tell them that space also is mind and the mind is invisible. I thought it was enough that they could grasp that. Well the look on their faces was something to behold. You could see they grasped what space was. They hugged each other and my granddaughter said, "Oh so that is what space is." And all the time they were thinking space was heaven only knows what. Outer space. Inner space. Water space, whatever. But they grasped that principle and they are five and eight. Now if they can grasp that, you can too today [laughter].

Now in this infinite space the mind is an instrument, a transparency. What is a transparency but an invisibility? These are Joel's terms: "Mind is a transparency." In this infinite invisibility, I, consciousness, conceptualize myself. I, consciousness, am. I am. And what am I? I create an image of myself, which the mind, because it is my instrument, is compelled to mirror back to me. The mind cannot think; the mind cannot create. It is like a river that you throw a pebble into and you see the circles created by the pebble. The river cannot do that; I have to throw that stone. Therefore, it is I who have the idea as consciousness. It is I who have the thought, good, bad, or indifferent. It is I who conceptualize a world based on two powers and put that into my mind and it reflects back to me. Now you will say, "How does that explain the same old things happening over and over and over again if mind cannot create?"

The Intellect

Then we come to intellect, which was an unfoldment I gave to this class nineteen years ago this month in October 1975. I have taken excerpts from that classwork to read to you today so that we can distinguish the difference between mind and intellect and realize why history keeps repeating itself.[*]

The intellect is the storehouse, the repository, of all of our human experiences. It too cannot create, but it is the bugaboo to our fourth-dimensional intuitive consciousness. It is that reasoning faculty we call the intellect which keeps throwing up the reasons why spiritual truth cannot be accepted into the mind. And I can best give this to you by taking these excerpts from that class which, as I said, was a breakthrough in consciousness.

It is not the mind which is holding us in humanhood. There is no conflict in my mind and your mind. Mind is an unconditioned avenue of awareness. It is an instrument of *I*, Consciousness, and is used by Consciousness for the purpose of manifesting or forming itself, Consciousness, and forming that Consciousness infinitely. It is the intellect, an adjunct of mind, that receives impressions and judges according to its memory of past experiences. Even our phrase, "He's losing his mind" is incorrect. He can lose his intellect, but he can never lose his mind. When we enter what also is called senility, what

---

[*] Editor's note: no attempt was made to delineate 1975 excerpted material.

shuts down? Not the mind. There are still pictures every-where. It is the intellect; the intellect has shut down. The individual has consciously or unconsciously closed the door on the intellect.

So it is the intellect that receives impressions and judges according to its memory of past experiences acquired through the five senses of taste, touch, sight, hearing, and smell. Now we know that anything that we can see, hear, taste, touch, and smell is not real. It has no substance and no power to support it—any picture, any image—and we see, taste, touch, hear and smell all of these images that are projections of the mind. The intellect compiles the memory of past experiences acquired through the five senses. The intellect is the store-house of human experience and academic learning and its judgments are better known humanly as common sense.

Now intuition is the sixth sense and it is to intuition that we turn to perceive true wisdom. Remember the things of God are unreasonable to the natural man and woman. Remember also that God says, "My thoughts are not your thoughts, and My ways are not your ways." Undoubtedly this is why it is said that a well-developed intellect is the strongest barricade to the kingdom of God.

You remember in the early years I used to say to a few of you, "You have the strongest intellect I have ever encountered" and you used to think I was paying you a compliment [laugh-ter]. Well, this is why it is necessary to become as a little child to receive spiritual awareness. It is certainly in the intellect that the personal sense of I is most heavily fortressed and this is the problem. This is where we live as human beings, this is where our I resides. We can't seem to transcend the intel-lect. We can't seem to get above it as a human being. Only in those rare times as a human being when we are quiet, when we are still, and the intuitive faculty works, do we transcend that intellect.

"As a Little Child"

You see, this is the difference now between mind and intellect: If you can grasp that your mind is out here, you already know you have transcended the mind because it can only be obedient to you. It is the intellect, the storehouse, that keeps throwing out these reasons why the intuitive information is not acceptable, because it works on logic. It works on past experience. Okay? In transcending the intellect, we do, and must, become as a little child for there is nothing established yet in a child's intellect to block the vision. There is no reason and there is no cause and there is no past experience to create doubt or fear.

All of you who have children have experienced their fearlessness when they were small, their disregard for rules and regulations, their total trust in not only you and me as parents, but other people as well. It's a beautiful thing to watch and it is heart-breaking to have to begin to train a child in this day and time not to trust people or not to go to visit people or to be fearful to go down the block. My little son, when he was two, thought the world was his oyster. There was nothing for him to fear. He thought nothing of going in and out of the neighbors' houses, using their potties, or whatever was available to him; he would say to me when I tried to teach him, "You just don't do things like that, you call first," "Well they love me. They love me." How could I explain to him that to them, he was just a pest coming in and out of their houses.

It is very difficult and yet this is what we as human beings do to our children so that by the time they are nine or ten, they are so conditioned to what we call the social graces—and that's a laugh—that they have had all the spirituality and the trust they came here with drummed out of them, and their intellect is now somewhat developed based on the conditioning you and I as parents and teachers drum into them. It is very difficult, this living between two worlds. You have to teach children the rules of society while at the same time showing them the reality, freeing them from that conditioning.

So we see there is no reason, no cause, and no past experience through which to create doubt or fear in a child's consciousness. A child held closely in the arms of its mother knows only perfect love because it has perfect trust. It has no fear. This dimension, being as a little child, is certainly an unknowing, unreasonable, unseeable, untasteable, unhearable, unfeelable, untouchable state of being. You cannot taste, hear, touch, see, or smell perfect trust. It is something discerned spiritually. And those of us who have experienced it are perfectly aware of this. In our adulthood, since we've been on the spiritual path, we have had these experiences where, as a little child, we are completely faithful, completely trusting, just as the woman was whose job was at stake and realized, "Well, I either have to stand on this or not." And so it performed that which was appointed for her.

This is the state beyond words and thoughts that initiated my healing work because I did not have a conditioned mind or intellect to interfere with that state of consciousness doing the healing beyond words and thoughts. I had a childlike state of consciousness. I had no metaphysics to get in my way, none whatsoever. But then to discover the principle that Joel and Jesus brought through, I had to study the letter of truth. Now what was I doing when I began to study the letter of truth? I was reconditioning my intellect.

I remember talking one day to a long-time Infinite Way student about twenty-three, twenty-four years ago, and something I said just suddenly clicked in her mind and she rose up and said, "Do you mean to tell me we've been brainwashed all these years?" And I answered, "Something like that." To her that was a terrible thing, the connotation of brainwashing. Well it's not brainwashing, but it is the reconditioning of your intellect over which you have dominion, and whether we consciously know that or not, it is exactly what we have been doing all the years we've studied the letter of truth.

Being Reborn

We are told when that job is finished, and the spirit of the truth is established, then it takes over and we no longer have to know the truth. So ask yourself, "Why don't I have to know the truth anymore?" Because I have a reborn intellect. My consciousness has been reborn of Spirit and that consciousness has retrained, through its dominion, the intellect and the mind. Now, the pictures begin to change. The mind is beginning to reflect back to me something different than ordinary human consciousness. I have a more harmonious life; I am more prosperous; I don't have bad health anymore. All kinds of good things begin to happen; everything begins to change.

Do you know the literal translation of repent means "change your mind?" Nobody can change the mind humanly. You and I cannot change the mind; we cannot spiritualize the mind until we rise to the fourth-dimensional consciousness. That is why as human beings, the intellect keeps pouring these same old notions back into the mind and we keep picking them up. Communication today might mean a fax, whereas it used to mean a hand-written note, but the principle hasn't changed. Human history keeps repeating itself: The pendulum swings to this extreme and back to the other extreme.

This state of "beyond words and thoughts," known in the East as the "void" and to others as the "vacuum," is created within us as an entry for spiritual consciousness. Without that vacuum and that void, spiritual consciousness cannot enter, cannot impress itself on the mind, cannot eradicate the human concepts we see reflected back to us. The mind as an avenue of awareness interprets this "beyond words and thoughts" as an extraordinary experience, because it is beyond the intellect. We have nothing humanly to relate it to. In fact, we cannot even bring it into the intellect, we cannot even bring spiritual consciousness or a description of spiritual consciousness into the intellect sufficiently to describe it, because there is no human language with which to describe it. It transcends, goes beyond, human consciousness, which means it has a language of its own which is perceived in the silence. And then the impact of that consciousness, that awareness of the fourth dimension, strikes the mind. Where else is it going to go? Mind fills all space and reflects back more of the true reality of that which it is. But it cannot be described. It can only be experienced.

It would be much like trying to explain what a human being is to your pet dog or cat. The fourth-dimensional consciousness cannot be explained to human consciousness. That is why Joel has emphasized that it must be experienced, and in order to experience it, we have to create this vacuum and this void through the continuous filling of our mind, keeping our mind and our intellect filled with truth until eventually the void is created and then the full impact of the fourth-dimensional consciousness can flow through, and it seems to change the picture. What has really happened is that in that void and that vacuum, in the space where the intellect is not ruling the mind, for that moment your *I* has transcended your intellect. It impacts the mind, and that we call repentance or changing your mind or a healing. Nothing has been healed. It was only a picture to begin with. The only difference is your changed consciousness is reflecting back a better picture.

Mind, an Infinite Instrument

The intellect then is that which is erroneously called the carnal, mortal, or human mind. It is the intellect that gives us the difficulties which oppose clear understanding. The mind is an infinite instrument of an invisible substance which forms images conceived by the I wherever it may be residing in consciousness. The intellect is a reservoir of human beliefs and concepts formed to accommodate the false sense of I. Another very important point here: It forms to accommodate the false sense of I because the real *I*, the reality of I, the spiritual *I*, does not need it. The spiritual *I* does not even need the mind. The mind is created by the spiritual *I* as an instrument simply to reflect back to itself that which it is. Actually, Consciousness itself is all and needs no help and no pictures, no nothing. As human beings we have mirrors where we can see reflected back to us our concept of ourselves. And that is what the mind is.

So this is an important point. The intellect is a reservoir of human beliefs and concepts formed to accommodate the false sense of I which has lost sight of its origin and oneness with the Source. In other words, as human beings we look to the intellect as our source, not God. You think about that for a minute. It's true. We see over and over the same suggestions, the same beliefs, and the same false information regarding good and evil, two powers. Over and over, that's all we get:

This is good and this is bad based on my past experience and my memory of former experiences, past lives, and academic training, and we believe it, and it stops us. That's what makes it the greatest barricade to spiritual consciousness; all of our faith and trust is in it.

Let's think of consciousness as the invisible, individual *I*, the Spirit which I am. The mind has no capacity to think or create and neither does the intellect. *I* think; *I* create. The mind is unconditional, unintelligent substance. It's like dough, like dough. Anything you think or I think, I create; the mind has to form it. It is your instrument. It belongs to you. We say, "my mind, your mind." It is your instrument. You are responsible for what you put in it. And you are responsible for what you reject. You have dominion over it.

It is a vast unconditioned unintelligent substance. The mind has no intelligence. Just think of all the attributes we've been attributing to mind all these years by human beings. The mind has no power, no intelligence. It is an invisible substance filling all space that we use to create our world, to become aware of a spiritual world. It is an avenue of awareness through which intuition functions. But what slows us down is that stinking thinking from the intellect. That is where we get caught up. Who was it that said, "I think, therefore I am"? The intellect loves that.

The mind then is a vast mirror reflecting to us only that which we can conceive—our concepts. We've heard the mind is the mirror of the soul, the eyes are the windows of the soul; well the mind is the dough into which we impress our concepts of ourselves. It is used by individuals at all levels of consciousness. These impressions on the mind appear as body, structure, material, and other forms of infinite variety. Even our five senses are conceptualized extensions of inner faculties. Don't we speak of hearing with the inner ear, seeing with the inner eye? These senses are extensions of spiritual ideas and are useful to us in this human experience, in this manifested experience. And so, they, also, are an appearance of mind. They are concepts. In our limited capacity, we use them. They are concepts, mental concepts. And why? Because this entire image is a mental image. This is not our real body. This is not our spiritual body. This is our concept of body which mind is reflecting back to us. But *I* govern it. I can speak into my mind from my spiritual, infinite capacity; I can say to it, "Peace, be still," and the minute I do that and feel that inner response, that inner release of pure spiritual substance, the picture changes.

Personally, Meg cannot give peace to anything. It is only from the height of spiritual awareness, that faith that we are talking about, that inner trust, that conviction, that I can close my eyes, and from that height, transcending the intellect, lifting my *I* up out of the intellect, knowing that I am speaking into the mind, "Peace!" And then I get my release and something happens in the mind.

Mind and the Intellect
~Session Two~

I *Transcends the Intellect*

THE INTELLECT WAS originally created as a faculty of discrimination, a discerning faculty, which enabled individuals to know the difference between the Creator and the forms of creation—that was its proper function. Intuition is the link or bridge to the Soul, which we know to be individual divine identity. As this faculty or sixth sense opens up, we are on the path to the fourth-dimensional consciousness, but we cannot get there except to cross that bridge. The intuitive faculty has to be opened. It is the faculty of the Soul and it is that through which we cross into fourth-dimensional consciousness. As we begin to rely more and more on this soul-sense, this inner faculty, we leave the intellect further and further behind. It seems obvious to me that humans' so-called descent occurred when they transferred their allegiance to the intellect and began to I-dentify with the mental images.

Except for brief flashes of intuition which are largely ignored by the intellect as unreasonable because we have no experience by which to judge them, individuals live and view the illusory patterns of this world in repetitive fashion. And that is why history keeps repeating itself. The intellect is limited. As we grow weary of this interminable wheel of sameness, the I begins to lift itself out of the intellect and somewhere, buried deep within, the intuition begins to function. For a moment, the intellect is still. The I ascends over the bridge of intuition and dwells briefly in the Soul.

This is where we are; we are dwelling briefly in the Soul. We are able through this bridge of intuition to dwell briefly in the Soul, but we are not in a place yet where we can maintain it consciously and continuously. And this is why we have to remember truth every day; we have to use the knowledge of truth to lift ourselves up to where we can have that inner door open so that the fourth-dimensional consciousness can flow into the mind and impact it.

You cannot always go within as we did a few minutes ago and make that immediate contact and have it flow out. It happens most of the time if you are a practitioner in particular. But if you've been working, or if you've been at the market, or you've been tending children all day or doing something seemingly in the outer, you cannot immediately close your eyes and reach that high estate. That's when the letter of truth comes into play. You are lifting your I out of your intellect. All day your I has been functioning in your intellect—at business, at school, wherever you may be—and you've been living with one foot in the human scene and with an inner ear attuned to the fourth dimension. So when you go into meditation, your objective is to leave this world, to leave the intellect, to rise into this other dimension and sometimes we have to gradually, for a few minutes, recondition the intellect until we can raise ourselves out of it and make this contact higher and higher. That's creating the void.

As the journey is accomplished more frequently through meditation, the I begins to assume dominion over the senses which are integral parts of the structural vehicle which is formed with the substance of mind for its experience on earth. The I transcends the intellect which remembers two powers and is eventually restored to its natural function of distinguishing between reality and illusion. The "man of earth" and the man of Christ are then reconciled and thereafter coexist with the Father, the all-Spirit or universal Consciousness. The world then is mind-formed. The instruction is to live in it but not be of it. Therefore, we cannot leave the mind; we can, though, understand its natural place and function in the scheme of things.

Images in the Mind

The I dwelling in the intellect has created images in the mind and ascribed power to them, labeling them good and evil. Remove the power and all that's left is the image, just like a picture on the wall. You remove the power, the label, from the form and the form is nothing, which is its real nature—nothing. The mind is nothing. The pictures we look at are nothing. They are mental images in thought. Mind is pure, unconditioned. There is no good and there is no evil in mind. It is an instrument of awareness reflecting back to us that which we are and that of which we are conscious. When we say "That which we are," ninety-nine times out of a hundred we immediately think personal: "That which I am." We think individual identity. We don't think I, consciousness. What is reflected back to us from the mind is I, consciousness, that of which I am aware.

It is not like looking into a mirror and seeing your human sense of self. It is not like seeing your appearance reflected back to you. It is seeing that which you are conscious of as yourself and it reflects back as an appearance, as a shadow. So the mind having no power and no intelligence cannot sustain the image. Only the *I* of your being and mine can breathe the bright breath of life into that picture and hold it in the mind.

This is what happens when people get sick. They think they are sick; they hold that picture of illness and there are some who just cannot let it go for one reason or another. You and I might not even see illness, but they cannot let it go. So it's the I, our individual I, that breathes life into the picture and holds it in the mind. And only that I can release it or that I can let it destroy me. If I give the picture qualities for good or evil, I am sustaining it by the power with which I have endowed it. For instance, the minute I withdraw my consciousness from the Study Center, the center would begin to dissolve, just as my human sense of this body would if I were making a transition.

The moment we withdraw power from any form, the appearance begins to dissolve. When you step in front of a mirror, you see an image. When you move away from the mirror, the mirror is blank. So who is projecting the image? Who is holding that image in the mirror? Well the mind works in the same way. The minute I turn away from the mind and turn within, the image is gone. So who is holding it? Who is sustaining it? There is no God in the human scene. Joel taught us this in 1954. What he means is there is no God in the human picture, because the picture has no intelligence, no wisdom, no substance, no consciousness. It's a picture, like this piece of paper; you would never give this piece of paper credit for being powerful. It is made of the substance of mind.

The men and women of earth direct their limited will and it works temporarily as a limited form, a limited concept. But the spiritual ideas of God can never be dissolved, because they are eternal and have the capacity to multiply as form. Human beings can direct their limited will and it works temporarily on the mind as a limited form, but anything made of God, anything created by God, is immovable, irrevocable. What God hath joined together no one can put asunder. And if you don't believe this, go to the mountains and sit there and try to move one mountain from one place to another or try to change the tides in the ocean or try to change a law such as like begets like. Anything that God has created is invincible. Individuals can only destroy their own concepts. So if lack and limitation and human beings or human conceptualized forms were made by God, they could not disappear, they could not be changed, right? Now I, in my true identity, and you in your true identity, are eternal, infinite, spiritual individuality, the children of God, the perfect idea of the creative Principle, but humanly, we are multiplied form.

A spiritual idea is one. Whenever you are looking into your mind and complaining about all the bad pictures you see and praising all the good pictures you see, bear in mind that I am one, and mind is my instrument to reflect back to me that which I am. So if I'm seeing human beings, then that's what I am. If I'm seeing good and evil, then that's what I am. But if I'm seeing the Christ, if I'm seeing the perfect, ideal child of God, even though I have to look through the appearance to look right into the eyes, then that's what I am. And more and more, your environmental pictures change and you begin to see harmonious relationships where dissension was. You begin to lose your fears around employment, income, companionship; all of this appears because when you realize the Christ, you realize all. That's everything. That's the ideal, perfect, spiritual idea of being. And so your world begins to change, and those individuals who cannot respond to that repentance, that changing of mind, will fade out of your consciousness.

No In-Betweens

Every day strong-willed individuals and groups manipulate the human scene. They send out subliminal propaganda as well as overt propaganda. And those who do not understand the mind as an instrument of consciousness pick up this misleading propaganda and begin to follow its instructions like sheep. Do you know there is no way we're going to be able to dissolve a universal drug problem until they stop advertising medical prescription drugs on television and the newspapers? There's no way. You can't. It's just like realizing the Christ. When you realize the total Christ, you've got it all. But you cannot realize a tenth of the Christ and you cannot be just a little honest; you're either honest or you're not. So you are either for drugs or you're against drugs. That's what Jesus said: "I don't want any in-betweens; you're either with me or you're against me. You cannot be a little bit for me."

This is why these addictions keep reappearing in the mind because they're being treated piecemeal in human consciousness. I think it was in 1954 when Joel first told us about subliminal propaganda. At that time, it was stopped. I have read only recently that now it is used a lot, in which case unsuspecting people who don't have your perspective wake up every morning and decide to go vacation in a place that they had no desire a week ago to visit or they decide to join a religious denomination in which they never had an interest. This is subliminal propaganda. Of course, we all know how frequently we will take on a cold or a headache that's being broadcast over the waves of the mind. This is all subliminal perception and this is the reason why the disciplines of The Infinite Way are so important and why, in my work with students one-on-one over the years, I have stressed these disciplines. You never get beyond using the disciplines or the letter of truth.

It is we who are dragged into the muck and mire of human consciousness every day and it is we who have to extricate ourselves from it and to assure ourselves every morning that as much as possible we will not be dragged into it. That is why when we wake up in the morning, before we get out of bed, we do the protective work. What are we doing when we do that protective work? We are taking dominion over our mind. We are declaring to the mind that nothing shall come nigh my dwelling place that is alien to the Christ. I have declared this to my mind out here. I don't need any protection when I know it and when I have instructed my mind, but what I am protecting myself from is being used by all of these false beliefs. It is up to me; God gave me this mind. God gave you this mind and gave you dominion over it and so it is up to you and to me to keep that mind pure and unconditioned and stay attuned to the fourth-dimensional consciousness through which our repentance comes, our redemption comes, and the mind changes and then reflects back to us more of the reality instead of the false beliefs we have entertained and stored in the intellect to trip us up at every moment.

There are people who don't want the world to be saved, who don't want a change of consciousness. All you have to do is look around you to see the masses just tripping along like little sheep following every suggestion—good, bad, or indifferent, and worse—believing that they haven't a choice and they don't. Only those who know this truth have that choice. But the higher we go, the more we become aware of the one Mind as an instrument of the supreme *I*, and we no longer accept the superimposed suggestions of humans; we reject these suggestions as serpentine whispers and turn within with the realization that no weapon formed against me shall prosper. That is, as long as I am dwelling in the secret place of the Most High, as long as I am recognizing God or creative Principle as the only power, and I am That.

Let's stop now for our noon meditation.

Deepening Understanding

Joel said the secrets of the mind, although having been revealed in the last century, would not be understood for another hundred years or so, and his book, *The Thunder of Silence*, would not be understood either for probably another century. And this certainly has proved to be true because over and over we study the processes of the mind, we study the principles under which the mind functions, and still we have not grasped its operation. As I said in the first session, my first unfoldment came thirty-two, thirty-three years ago and I'm still getting a deeper and deeper understanding of it. No unfoldment on the mind can be considered the ultimate; no unfoldment on any aspects of the mind can be considered the absolute truth, because creative consciousness is constantly unfolding.

Remember, the principles never change but it is our individual understanding of them that changes. This is what we mean when we speak of the evolution of human consciousness. There is no such thing as evolution of human consciousness in the mental way in which it is meant. And in spiritual consciousness, we are simply coming into the awareness of that which is, of that which we already are. In the mental world they speak of evolving consciousness and even in our spiritual work, in our Infinite Way teaching, Joel speaks of the three degrees of spiritual evolution; but as we develop this higher understanding, both individually and as groups, we are in what would mentally be called a process of evolution.

Still we must keep our inner *I* on the goal of spiritual illumination rather than evolution. We are going for illumination.

Here again is another thing that we have to take into consideration: illumination. While illumination is a spiritual experience, a oneness with the creative Force, the one Creator, and results in a consciousness of omnipresence, omnipotence, and omniscience, we still are aware of this experience through the instrument of the mind. This is why it is so difficult to grasp. Earlier I said that Consciousness does not even need the mind, because Consciousness is pure and Consciousness is conscious of itself. But it evidently has created the mind as the mirror of itself, so as to reflect back its own being.

Considerations like this are like the Zen koan and the parables of Jesus and the contradictions in all spiritual literature, which are deliberate. They are deliberately conceived and used in all spiritual teaching, and that is so the intellect, which is such a strong barrier, can be circumvented. The intellect rejects anything unlike itself. So if you dump a Zen koan into it or before its eyes, such as, "What is the sound of one hand clapping?" that throws the intellect into a frenzy, because there is no logic to that; there is no reason to that.

When Jesus talked about the parables and gave his analogies, the intellect had no basis for comparison, so the intellect could be circumvented. In other words, you can go under it, you can go over it, or around it, but don't try to go through it, because then you fight it. This is why we become so frustrated with the letter of truth because it does not make sense. It is contradictory. That is not us. The I that we are is striving mightily to grasp the knowledge of spiritual being, but the intellect blocks us because it says to us, "This does not make sense, reject; this does not make sense, reject." So the I of us just keeps plodding and plodding.

I'll share with you an experience I had during the first couple of years of my study because it is indicative of what has to happen in our pressing forward toward this light we intuitively know is there. Sensing this block in my consciousness, I was thrown into this battle between the flesh and the Spirit where I wanted to know, but at the same time had set up that which prevented me from knowing called the "enemy at the gate," which is personal sense, a false sense of myself that was standing in the way. I had put into this storehouse, this intellect, all of these false beliefs, and it had built up its own ego. I was trying to get through, yet was fighting it at the same time. I was working diligently at the time with Joel's *The Thunder of Silence*, working with all the proper motives and proper desires to know God aright to understand spiritual truth. Still, I kept running up against my intellect until I was ready to scream. This went on for weeks on end and all through it I was asking, "What is the mind? What is the mind? I've got to know what the mind is." In this particular case, what I was striving for was not to know what the mind was, but to understand one *I*—oneness. I was in duality. I had absolute faith there was a universal *I*, but I had equally absolute faith that there was an individual I. And I felt two.

I was working for weeks and on this particular winter night the children were in bed and my husband was out of town. I was so exasperated, so frustrated, I was about to tear my hair out. In retrospect, I see what had happened. The intellect had just been thrown into that hysterical frenzy, because I wouldn't give up. I was hammering at the door. And all of a sudden, I felt I just couldn't stand it anymore and there was a kind of giving up, a sudden relaxing, and at that moment, I heard something with my inner ear. It was a crack, like an eggshell breaking, and through that crack, the truth of oneness entered my consciousness.

"You Are Looking at It"

It was not long after that it came to me: "What is the mind?" And the answer, "You are looking at it." Then eventually, the unfoldment of the intellect as the demon at the gate, and it was like my mind cracked. People talk about losing their mind or breaking their mind or cracking their mind, but later, with the unfoldment on the intellect, I realized it was the intellect that cracked, not the mind, because Consciousness is the only creator and mind forms. Consciousness is the essence of all creation, but mind forms, and what mind forms is called matter. But these forms in matter cannot be multiplied, neither does the intellect multiply.

Earlier I said our human sense of I is situated in the intellect and the intellect keeps producing the same forms over and over, the same human concepts over and over. What seem to us like different forms—as I said like going from the handwritten note to the fax machine—is really the same form. It is matter and it is limited. But when God creates, it is indestructible, and it can multiply. This is the principle behind humanhood. This is the principle behind you and me: what we look at is multiplied form.

There is one spiritual idea of humankind which Jesus exemplified as the perfect man. He came into the mind-formed world to exemplify to us God's spiritual idea of the perfect man who came to show us that he was the way; he was the life; he was God incarnate in the imaged world. He was the Word made flesh; the *I am* made flesh as individual being, which is what each of us is supposed to aspire to—that is, the Christ, the perfected being.

Now, in our humanhood that is what it seems; we are evolving toward that mind which was in Jesus Christ. In reality, we already are that mind. Going through the intellectual process of purifying the intellect, we are going through what mentally is called an evolutionary process in consciousness—going from the human to the Divine. Deep down, though, we know we are already the Divine, because Jesus has personified it, and what we are looking at is just the multiplied form, because man, spiritual man, is already perfect and what we look at are the mental images multiplied. I and Jesus are one and the same. I and Joel are one and the same, and if we could accept that, the images would disappear, because the images are just that—nothing. It's a dream world. Another teacher says that in reality, we're off somewhere else doing something else. We're just dreaming all this. And you ask, "Well, why don't you wake me up?" Why? I mean nothing is wrong, you see? Why should I wake you up? I can look at you and I can see how you are struggling. This is your intellect struggling to understand and grasp what I'm saying, because this is a very important class and you are too far along for it to be rejected.

So essentially, what this class is, is a Zen koan, a conundrum, a parable. Some of you called me last week and said, "I'm getting awfully agitated." Well this is why you were getting agitated, because this is a work that cannot be solved with your intellect. You are either going to have to transcend that intellect and leave it behind, at least momentarily, and get out of the way and let the reality of you, your Christhood, deal with it and purify the intellect and bring you into the realization of who you are, or you are going to continue to fight the battle between the flesh and the Spirit and be in the middle of it. Your little I will be trying to do something, trying to solve the problem, trying to be something, when essentially all there is, is God, and God is the I of you, and God is the I of me. That being so, God is the perfect creator.

We trust the sun to come up every morning. We trust the moon to come up at night. We trust the grass to grow and the tides to be correct. We trust all of those things universally to this Creator and this Sustainer and we cannot trust ourselves? This is the little child. We cannot trust ourselves to be led and guided and fed and sustained and maintained by the very creative force that put us here, that lives our life? Can't we understand, can't we transcend the intellect sufficiently to know that were there not a God we couldn't even be here, we couldn't be alive? Does it make sense? Does it make spiritual sense or even common sense in this case, to believe in a God that would let us suffer, that would let us go hungry, that would let us kill each other, rape each other, vandalize each other? That's the dream! Those are the human forms and they will continue as long as there is a belief in personal sense, a belief in a selfhood apart from God, a belief that you and I are something of ourselves, a belief really that we are greater than God. This is the danger.

Now, you are all at a place in consciousness where you are not too far away for a mind breakage of your own, where one of these days some of you are going to have this experience of realization of who *I* am. And when you do, it's going to blow your mind. It's not going to break your mind; it's going to blow your mind. It's going to blow your intellect to smithereens. At that time, what you will be standing on is your illuminated Mind purified by the letter of Truth. The mind is the illuminator, reflection, mirror.

Mind and the Intellect
~Session Three~

Only One

I CANNOT KNOW MYSELF without knowing you. I cannot know myself without knowing God and I cannot know God without knowing myself. There is only One, One, One! That is the song you should sing, the story you should preach—One, One, One. The mind has no power to keep this from you. The mind has to be obedient. It is your instrument. It has to be obedient to your instructions. If you instruct it, "I and the Father are one, and all that the Father hath is mine," there has to be some response but not if you're doing this with your intellect. We can read the words but with no conviction, no faith behind those words, the form cannot be multiplied. Then it just goes into the intellect and you get the same old merry-go-round over and over and over again. We get organized churches, we get cults, we get the white and the black brotherhoods, because it's all done in the mental realm.

But when you have spiritual conviction that this is so by virtue of "my Father within hath told me so," my intuition has spoken to me, the still small voice, which is intuition, hath spoken to me and I know this is so. I can say to you that I know this unfoldment on mind is the truth because it's demonstrable; over many years it has been proven in my experience. But I cannot say to you that this is all the truth and I cannot say to you that another teacher, an author, a revelator might not come along and make this unfoldment obsolete.

No person, with the exception of that perfect man, the purest Jesus, can say "I am the way, I am the truth, and I am the life." In fact, I don't even feel a person in the human form, with the exception of those who have fully attained to conscious union with God, should be called a spiritual teacher—teachers of spiritual truth, yes—truth they can prove. But "spiritual teacher" has too strong a connotation in our language and it could be misleading. So when we help others and we are called teachers, let us call ourselves teachers of spiritual truth rather than a spiritual teacher. Certainly, we are all spiritual beings, but in a spiritual world there are no teachings; no teachers are needed. So while we are here in this form, let us choose our words as carefully as we can so as not to offend the intellect, but to circumvent the intellect.

There is a question here: "How does 'God is the substance of all form' go with 'all the forms we see are nothing as reflections of the mind'?"

The Substance of All Forms

I was just explaining that: Truth, God, becomes the essence and substance of all forms and the form can then be multiplied because that's the reality of it. The mental forms that just keep going round and round because there is no *I* directing them are products of the intellect and they do not multiply; they cannot be multiplied. This is the principle behind Jesus multiplying the loaves and fishes and the principle behind the one individual in multiplied form on earth. This is multiplied form. A spiritual idea such as supply can come in multiplied form when it is spiritually realized, but mentally it cannot be multiplied.

So what this student is essentially asking is "What is the difference between the Word made flesh which is permanent, and the flesh that is here today and can be thrown into the oven tomorrow?" There is a wonderful series on that in the 1954 Practitioner's Class* that I think thoroughly explains the difference between the two fleshes. You see that too is a conundrum, a Biblical poser, one of many, to throw the intellect off kilter.

Once the mind becomes permeated with truth and the intellect is purified, then the truth becomes the essence of the forms of mind. That is the flesh that is indestructible; that is the form that is indestructible, like the mountains, the oceans, the planets, etc. But the forms we live with day in and day out—like clothing, images of bodies, automobiles, houses, multitudinous infinite forms that we see—are destructible. They not only can be destroyed, they can be changed. The images are changed constantly as the intellect provides more and more complicated ways to change the forms to keep you entertained and attached, to keep you interested. Can you see that a little bit?

In Chapter 6, "Unconditioned Mind" of *The Thunder of Silence*, Joel says, "Human experience is in reality the perfect mind, your mind and my mind, which manifests as perfect being and body, but which as human experience is influenced

---

* Recording 0095A: 1954 Portland Practitioner Class – "Flesh and Flesh." Available for purchase from www.joelgoldsmith.com.

by the knowledge of good and evil. The belief in two powers is the essence of what is called the carnal mind." As was presented earlier about withdrawing power from the picture, if we didn't have concepts imposed upon us by the intellect, which once again is the reservoir of all of the false beliefs in the world, if we didn't have those beliefs—let's say of beautiful, ugly, fat, thin, the racial beliefs and all of that—imposed upon our consciousness, we would look at each other with absolutely pure love. There would be no judgments of what we looked like; there would be no judgments of how we were groomed or what our nationality or our race is. There would be no judgments at all. When there are no judgments what do you have? Perfection.

Now I'd be willing to bet that some of you, when you think of the word perfection, may think of the most beautiful person you have ever seen in the world or the most beautiful building or the most beautiful geographical location, and you see, that's your intellect handing you a picture that's already been conceived. But if you stand perfectly still and say "Father, let me see what perfection is to *you*," then something unbelievable, extraordinary, will impress itself upon the mind. You would have the essence of it within your consciousness, so that like God, you wouldn't need the mind, you wouldn't even sit around to see it manifest because you would have the essence of it. And then when it manifested you would realize that's the added thing, that's the reflection of my experience, but you would have no judgment and no attachment to it, because what you have experienced is that the essence can form itself over and over and over again. It can multiply the form, whereas, if you take that concept from the intellect that is being offered you, you just have one thing that is here today and gone tomorrow and it cannot multiply.

Again from Chapter 6, Joel says:

Mind forms its own conditions of matter, body, and form. Mind does not *create*, mind *forms*. Creation is already complete—spiritual, eternal, and perfect—but our mind, depending on its conditioning, forms and interprets our human experience on this plane. If our mind is completely free of the judgment of good and evil, then Spirit forms its own image and likeness through the mind as happy, harmonious, and successful living. If mind is conditioned by judgments of good and evil, mind is not a clear transparency, and in proportion to its conditioning will experiences of good and evil take place in our lives.

Do you see? He's clear as a bell here. It is just that our understanding was not ready for this many years ago. And it's a day-by-day process which results in the mental definition of it as evolution. What's really happening is that we are slowly awakening to reality and we are slowly taking dominion over this instrument which was given to us for our use. As we begin to understand that, then we understand the body. We understand that the body is a form of life. All mental forms are called material. But actually, material forms are made out of mind, so mind and matter are one and the same thing.

When you look at the images and you are aware of this, you can instantly say "This is a mental picture. It is not the reality." And if you want to see the reality, then go within and ask: "I know this is not true. I know that is what my senses tell me, but this is just a mind-formed picture. This is just an image. It has no substance, no power, no law to sustain it. Let me go to the source of my consciousness, of my awareness, of my creativity, and see what's really here." If you are looking at a person then you might hear, "This is My beloved Son in whom I am well pleased."

Now just saying that to you doesn't mean a thing. But when you touch that inner dimension, that fourth-dimensional Consciousness, and it says that to you, there is also an instantaneous knowing of what that means at the moment it's spoken. So once again, you don't have to look at the picture to see if it's going to change because you have the essence. It does change. It has to change, because *I* has spoken. But you, as the mediator between the natural man and God, do not need the proof.

This happens many times in healing work and it is often misunderstood, because Joel has taught us that as long as that picture is there and someone is calling you for help, whether you have had this inner experience or not, you keep going back within. But there have been times in my work when I have had this inner vision or this inner revelation or experience and the patients may have called back for two days and I never did another piece of work because I knew it was done; I knew the truth. But sometimes in time and space it takes that long for them to respond to the experience. That's on this plane. Actually, all healings are instantaneous because when God speaks, the earth melts—the earth, meaning the mind, the mental picture.

Joel continues:

> When we are faced with a problem at any level, we must first remember that the substance of the visible universe is unconditioned mind which is the instrument of pure immortal Being, Essence, Substance, and Reality, and its formations are also unconditioned, because they are mind itself appearing as infinite form.
>
> Mind, unconditioned and having no qualities of good or evil, is the substance of all that is visible; and all that is, is as unconditioned as the mind which is its basis. If this were not

true, it would be impossible for our state of consciousness to produce changes in what is called the material universe.

Our Conditioned Intellect

All right, let's take this sentence: "Mind, unconditioned, and having no qualities of good or evil, is the substance of all that is visible." Now, let us look at our bodies. All these bodies are mind formed. Let's accept the mind is unconditioned substance. It's pure as the driven snow. It's space. When you look at the mind, all you see are the forms in the mind. You don't see the mind. But every one of these forms is made of this same pure, invisible substance as our bodies are and our homes and all structure.

It is our conditioned intellect that makes the judgment as to whether we like that form in the mind or not, or whether we feel that it's good or it's evil or it's indifferent or it's pretty or it's ugly or whatever. It is our conditioned intellect. Now individually, this is created through our background, our upbringing from babyhood, our academic training, all of these—cultural, environmental—everything that we have been brought up in. This is what causes the judgment because we have allowed the intellect to accept that conditioning and now we are responsible for it. The intellect is like a naughty child when we begin to purify it by putting truth into it and so you have to take it firmly by the hand and take dominion over it. And every time it throws up a judgment to you, and it's very subtle as you all know, you can be trapped in so many different ways because you are habitually accustomed to the intellect telling you what you are to think and how you are to live, and what judgments you are to make, and what to wear even. It accepts all of the fashionista rules imposed on us. It has people spending hundreds of thousands of dollars a year, individually, on changed fashions every season whether they're pretty or ugly. It is the same with advertising drugs and with "shop till you drop," and "I'm helping the economy; I'm going out and spending whether I've got it or not." But the intellect accepts all this. It keeps you busy. All of that is imposed on you.

The mind, though, is pure. The mind is unconditioned. As we look at all the forms, including the forms of our bodies and our homes and our employment and our companions, we have to realize that these images are as pure as the mind itself and just stop. If you are sincere, whether you can close your eyes or not, just throw it back into consciousness. "I would really like to see what is here. I know that this is an intellectually imposed image on my consciousness, and I know it's a picture, and I'm not involved with it; I'm not attached to it. I would just like to see what is really behind it, because behind every form there is a reality, there is a message, and I would like to see what's really there." Then if you are still enough, something beyond anything your intellect could dig up will come to you. And then the essence of that, which is Consciousness, a higher, deeper, awareness, which is the only thing that controls and creates with the mind, will register on that mind and you will get a different picture. Either that one will dissolve and a brand new one will come, or that one will change, because mind is the instrument of the Creator, and mind is pure, and mind is unconditioned.

The Illuminator

Now we have the Trinity: I, the Father, the universal I; I, the Son, the Christ, individual being; and I, the Holy Ghost. And what is the Holy Ghost? The Illuminator. The Holy Ghost is the union, the knowledge, the experience of union between individual being and God. And the mind illuminates that—the Word made flesh. That is your trinity. There are many trinities, but this is the one I am talking about. God the Father, universal Omnipresence; God the Son, the individualized Christ, the only Son of God and the Illuminator which is the instrument through which God the Father creates and God the Son creates. And the reason we are doing what we call finding our way back to the Father's house is because individually we have used up our substance.

As was pointed out earlier, we transferred our allegiance to the intellect and let it make our decisions for us instead of staying connected to our Source which is infinitely creative, which never leaves us wanting, and which is the trunk of the tree of which we are a branch. We've been stuck in the mind, attached to the images, attached to the concepts of supply, of health, of wealth, of happiness, of family, all of these false concepts. Not a one is true. Not a one. They are all lies. *I* am supply. *I* am health. *I* am wealth. *I* am companionship. It is all within me. It is stored up within my consciousness, not my intellect. And the way I express it is through the mind. I have, I am. I am that *I am*. And so, I have dominion over this mind which is my beautiful unconditioned instrument just to pour, to give, to create, to share. You cannot get anything back. You are the creator.

The mind will form whatever you create, but you just have to remember that there is only one, there is only one. If you use it for selfish, indulgent purposes, then you will be right down in the pigsty again. That is exactly what happened before. And if you use the mind to harm your neighbors, instead of assuming the responsibility for your own formations, you can take from your neighbor who is unaware of this, but it will be temporary; it will rebound on you because there is only one. All these images out here are you, facets of your own consciousness. No point in trying to run away from them or in trying to destroy them or wishing they'd go away. They have to be redeemed. Sorry to tell you this. They have to be redeemed, and in your redemption of them, your consciousness changes.

When Joel made his transition in 1964, I was still a young student, and I still needed a visible teacher. There were none available to me that I felt I could be at-one with. So what happened was I became the teacher. Now you think about that. When a teacher was needed, I became the teacher. And it is I who have benefited from my own teaching all these years more than the students. As Joel used to say, the reason The Infinite Way work came to him was because he was the fellow who needed it the most. Well these students came to me because I was the fellow who needed them the most. Do you see? The spiritual life is the direct reverse of the mental reflection of what you think of as the human scene: the direct reverse. When you look in the mirror, your left arm looks like your right and vice versa.

And so, when you're looking into your mind, remember it's a reflector and it's the direct opposite of the reality. But ladies and gentlemen, this is your mind. I'm as sure of it as anything I could possibly be sure of, and it is that knowledge that has demonstrated itself in my experience over and over and over again. The mind is pure and unconditioned and you have dominion over it.

"Because I Said So"

The next step is the realization that you also have dominion over that adjunct which is called the intellect. You don't have to do anything to it. You don't have to fight it. You don't have to struggle. You have to transcend that. You have already transcended the mind, remember? You never have been in it. You just thought you had and you are not in the intellect either, but you really think you are and you are letting it control you. So this is what you purify. This is what you say no to, like a naughty child. "No, I'm sorry you cannot have that candy today. No, I've changed my mind about this." And, if it argues back merely say, "Because I said so."

It always works: "Because I said so. That's why." It will always ask you why—"Why do you want to do this?"—to make you doubt. Another thing you can do when it's speaking to you is to ask it, "Who is speaking, please?" It shuts right up. It's just a matter of your taking your natural God-given authority. The same thing applies to the body. If you keep your mind filled with pornography and violence and lust and all those good things in humanhood, then that's what you are going to experience. You've got to remember, it's your responsibility to keep your mind clear, and that way you have dominion over it. That's the purpose, of course, of reading all the books, listening to the tapes, coming to class, associating with each other, because you are in an atmosphere and this is going into your mind. It's so obvious. It's no secret any more.

> Matter is matter only to the material state of consciousness, but once we rise to a mental state of consciousness matter is not matter, but mind. Mind is the essence and substance of which matter is formed and it appears to us as form or effect. Mind is the principle, the life, and the law of all material and mental form. *

But consciousness is the principle of mind. I'm reading that. It's going straight into the mind. You can see that. The difference, you have to remember, is if I'm just reading that

---

* Chapter 5, "Transcending Mind," *The Thunder of Silence.*

with no understanding of what I'm reading, that's all it is: just words with no more substance and no more power to form the truth in the mind than this glass of water. But if I read it with conviction and the consciousness is there of what I'm reading, then it goes right into the mind and it can be multiplied and here is the proof.

> Mind, unconditioned—infinite, eternal mind—is the substance of being, body, business, politics, government, industry, finance, art, and literature. This mind and its formations are neither good nor bad: They are unconditioned, eternal being, and that which we behold as an erroneous condition or circumstance is not of mind or its formations, but is the universal belief in good and evil, [held in your intellect] which is termed devil or carnal mind. *

Now, we are in danger even by naming the intellect of having something that we've got to overcome or something that's got to be done away with, just as we were in danger with mortal mind and the devil and carnal mind.

The day came when I realized very clearly that there was no carnal mind. What a beautiful realization that was for me: "Oh goodness, I don't have to do anything about that!" For so long I had been saying, "Well, that's the carnal mind, and we have to overcome that, and this is what we are dealing with here, the carnal mind." In Christian Science it's always, "This is mortal mind," so that was something that had to be overcome. Well I don't want that to happen with the intellect. I want you to realize exactly what it is, that it's just nothing claiming to be something. I don't want you to envision a storehouse out here with all these beliefs hanging out, because that can get you into trouble; it will give you something to overcome.

------

* Chapter 6, "Unconditioned Mind" *The Thunder of Silence.*

Taking Dominion

All you have to do is to take dominion over it and be on your toes. When Jesus said it takes twenty-four-hour vigilance, he wasn't joking. He meant it, and that's what we have to do. So you cannot forgo your discipline. Don't be egotistical to think that you've come so far that you can stop your protective work in the morning, that you can stop your meditative work. One teacher says meditation is "the ignition" and then you act. Well, that's true, and I love that phrase, "it's the ignition." But I have found also in my experience that it is my lifeline, that I am not empowered as yet; I have not fully attained; I am not empowered to just close the door and say, "Okay, I've got it now, and I don't have to deal with God anymore." That is the most dangerous place in your initiation: when you glimpse or realize that God is your being, that you are empowered from on high to create your own world and you know this, and you know there is only one, and you don't have to take anything from anybody anymore. It's all within you. You don't abuse anybody and you don't let anybody abuse you, and no back talk and nobody telling you what to do or anything else. Then you are in danger of thinking you are God and that you don't need God anymore. And you could not be more wrong.

There is a God. It is the creator of the universe and it is greater than we are. But as its offspring, we have been given dominion, as in the first chapter of Genesis, over everything as far as we can see—over our mind, over our body, over our lands, over our consciousness—as far as we can see belongs to us, which means as much as we are aware of, the mind forms. That is our world. But we don't become attached to it because we realize that the essence of it is that which I am, which is spiritual consciousness. And that which I am is one with the Universal and that is the source of what I am. So that can never be cut off and in your practice of this, you will never be tempted to do anything but love your neighbor as yourself. You will quickly come to realize that whatever you have does not belong to you. The earth is the Lord's and the fullness thereof.

As Joel says, we should be transfer agents, that it belongs to God, that we should never be afraid to let anything go and we should be so grateful that we have had this experience where we now are a transfer agent. We can just let it flow through, holding on to nothing. I don't mean being stupid or wasteful or poor managers of your income or anything, but whatever demand is made upon you, you are able to say, "Yes, I can. I can do all things through Christ. I can answer any demand." Nothing is impossible with God, nothing. What makes it seem impossible is our little selfish demands and our feeling of inadequacy. If we could make the leap, wow! We would be in the arms of the peerless Jesus tonight because we are that, and that's where your faith comes in.

"In the Surrender of Personal Will"

There have been occasions when people have stood on these principles to great sacrifice of personal sense, personal fear, and that's what it takes. That's what crucifixion is. You are not going to get through this without dying to personal sense. You cannot take your humanhood with you into the kingdom of God. Many students fall by the wayside or never move forward because they are trying to spiritualize their humanhood. We are clearly told in all the spiritual literature of the world that we leave it behind. We die to the old man. We are reborn of Spirit, which means the non-attachment to the forms and to the concepts of this world, because this *is* the kingdom of God. We are not going to go anywhere. It is just a different perception, a different way of looking at the universe and each other, a realization that we are one. We are one and whatever I think about you, I'm thinking about me.

My sins are sins of commission or omission. If I'm thinking wrong things about you, if I am bad-mouthing you, then it's going to come back to me. I'm doing it to myself and it will come back magnified to such a degree that I won't be able to miss it. And if I am refusing to share with you, then that produces lack in my life, a lack of whatever it is I'm refusing to share.

One more thing I'll read to you: "In the surrender of personal will, this unconditioned mind can operate in us and through us." (Ch. 6) Don't try to manipulate the mind. The minute you do, you are in your humanhood. Don't try to outline. Don't try to make it do what you want it to do. Don't try to make anybody else do what you want them to do. It's very easy to do once you know the secrets of the mind. But don't do it. Surrender your personal will. It's always, "Thy will be done," the spiritual *I* of your being, and then be still and let it function. As long as we condition mind with beliefs of good and evil, we will bring forth good and evil in proportion to our faith or our belief. As you become convinced in your heart, so is it unto you. It is all a matter of conditioning and you can condition yourself for good or for evil, but when you leave the realm of conditioning, then you are in that spotless area, the realm of that mind which was in Jesus Christ: spotless, pure, and no-judgment.

I'm not going to tell you you've got strong intellects because you haven't anymore, we've broken them down. But you are all intelligent and you can see that this is the truth. This is the truth. But hearing it and agreeing with it or even questioning it is not going to do it for you. It is practice. It is,

"Ye shall know the truth, and the truth shall make you free." It's not me or your neighbor, it is "ye," and a teacher cannot do this for you any more than a teacher can eat and sleep for you. A teacher can show you the way, point the way, share everything that a teacher has, but you have to do the work. And nothing keeps us from this attainment except mental inertia and a superficial welfare system: You apply for help and you get it, then you want to live off of it the rest of your life and that just does not work. Sooner or later supply stops, health problems come, everything happens if students do not progress. If, sooner or later, they do not become independent of the teacher and on the same level of consciousness as the teacher, then the teacher's consciousness, for no reason that the teacher knows, stops benefiting the students.

There's some built-in safety factor for the student. Yesterday when I came to a standstill with this class, (It's been a mind-boggling experience for me to try to bring it through in words that you could grasp and in the spirit that you could grasp without upsetting you too much.) there was a vacuum when I got through. It was just like a hush and into it the voice spoke and it said, "Well, I don't know what else you can do. But thank God you don't have a well-developed intellect, or it would be in hysteria by now!" I started to laugh and it laughed too. All of a sudden I thought, "Okay, this is the best I can do. That's all that matters."

Practice is the Preparation

You see with the student, this practice is the preparation. This is what we have to do. For almost three weeks now I have been pouring all this into my mind, keeping my intellect busy over here trying to reject and agree or reason or whatever, and making headway, but just keeping it going. That's what each one of us has to do. You cannot let up. Then I came to a place where I knew that this was all I could do. I had kept my mind filled with this principle. I had kept my heart filled with it. I had practiced it diligently for these three weeks without a letup; I had been hammering it into the consciousness of everyone I have talked with. So now, it is Sunday, I'm at the end of it. I can rest.

And you know, when that happens, you hear, "Okay, I will take over now," and you don't have worries anymore. You might be a little nervous that you don't have the vocabulary to bring it through, and I'm always nervous about that. But you know the Spirit is going to be there and you know that if the students are prepared to receive it in Spirit, they will grasp it by transcending the intellect. And you are grasping this, if you are grasping it at all, at a higher level than the mental. You are in spiritual consciousness at this moment.

Thank you so much.

OCTOBER 1994
ATLANTA STUDY CENTER CLASSES

Spiritual Healing, Spiritual Supply

Supply Is Spiritual Discernment

GOOD MORNING! Well, I stayed awake most of the night worrying whether you'd come back today or not, [laughter] or you slept it off. Thank you! But to sum up yesterday's message, we learned that consciousness creates, the mind forms, and the intellect, which is an aspect of mind or a facet of mind or an adjunct of mind, is the interpreter. And it is important that we have that concrete in our consciousness today before we go on to spiritual supply. Consciousness creates, the mind forms, and the intellect, the conditioned intellect, is your interpreter. There is a wonderful tape on the mind given by Joel called, "Mind is a Transparency."[*] Of course, there are several, but this one has recently come to our attention and we think it is probably the best we have heard and the clearest.

Well as our friend Yogi Berra says, "It's déjà vu all over again." Here we go once again on "supply." After fifty years of The Infinite Way you would think that no Infinite Way

---

[*] Recording 0496A: 1962 London Special Class – "Mind is a Transparency." Available for purchase from www.joelgoldsmith.com.

student would ever again have to have a class on supply, but it keeps coming up and coming up. So today maybe we can have it presented to us a little differently, so we can grasp the difference between spiritual supply and material supply, which seems to be the bugaboo with every student who asks for help with supply. Always when students or patients ask for help with supply, they mean money, and here is your intellectual interpretation of supply: money, a home, a job, all of which are human interpretations of the real meaning of supply.

Now spiritual supply is spiritual discernment, spiritual discernment of a spiritual principle. It has nothing whatever to do with our intellectual concepts of supply. Our intellectual concepts are what form in the mind when consciousness realizes, discerns, the principle of spiritual supply.

So here we have consciousness creates, mind forms, and the conditioned intellect interprets that to us in whatever way our human need seems to be. Let's say we have a lack of some kind and we go within to discern the principle, what I call "going for the principle"; let's bypass all the concepts and go for the principle. What *is* supply? In reality, what is supply? You know what its forms are and that again is the flesh that is here today and gone tomorrow. What we want, though, is permanent supply. We don't want a bank account today and barrenness next week. We want a consciousness of supply; we want to know the principle behind supply. So we go for that principle.

To this end once again, we study the letter of truth, we follow all guidelines to demonstrating supply, we accept gradually that "I and the Father are one and all that the Father hath is mine," so whatever I lack, or seemingly lack, must come through me. When you are young students, and even when we are older students, (and I still do this) you clean out your closets several times a year and give articles of clothing and household goods away that you don't use or that you can part with; you give to charity, you tithe, you share with each other and if you lack companionship, you understand that I have to be companionable. We have gone over all this year in and year out.

Whatever I seem to be lacking, I must be an instrument through which it flows. If I am looking for respect, I have to give respect; if I am looking for accolades, I have to give accolades; if I am looking for praise, I have to give it; if I am looking for love, I have to give it. All of these are forms of supply and a method by which we can open ourselves up and let the imprisoned splendor escape. So for years, we practice this principle as we know it intellectually and we do it from the within to the without. Now what we don't realize is that without the discernment behind that practice, that's the flesh that is here today and gone tomorrow.

Supply: A Deeper Level

You will, in the human scene, have come back to you that which you have given out. That is a law. But as I explained to you yesterday, that your five senses are extensions of inner spiritual faculties, so is this law of "cast your bread upon the waters." What we do as human beings is follow the letter of truth and practice the letter of truth with the idea in mind we are practicing spiritual principle. Then we have to go higher. We have to go for the principle itself, go for the discernment at a deeper level of consciousness.

There have been people who have tithed for years and years and years and have not realized wealth. Tithing is a spiritual principle but not at the level we think of it, not at the church level, not at the monetary level; the money that we tithe is the practical action behind the principle, it is not the principle itself, you see. It is like everything else. What is out here is conditioned; the forms are conditioned by our intellect which is the interpreter, so we get a glimpse of the principle of supply; we say, "Oh boy, tithing, that's the principle" and our mind interprets that as money, which is fine if you have got the principle behind it. But the money you cast out there without spiritual discernment is going to gradually dry up. Just as I said to you yesterday, you may for some years get healings and live under the consciousness of a teacher or practitioner, but all of a sudden it stops. That is what I call a built-in safety factor, to keep the student from being dependent on princes—"Put not your faith in princes"—to keep the students from being dependent on anyone or anything outside of themselves.

That is what happens in this principle of tithing. We get complaisant with the idea that we are giving money to this and money to that and that is our supply: "I'm demonstrating supply because I'm giving," and all of a sudden, we go broke. "Well my goodness, what's happening here? I've been tithing all these years, I've been doing what I thought was right." You see how the intellect interprets tithing to you? That brings us up short. And we ask, "Now what?" Well now we have to go to a deeper level of understanding of that principle of tithing.

The discernment, the spiritual discernment, the inner wisdom, the inner understanding of the truth of being, is the bread you cast upon the waters, which comes back to you earmarked to be delivered to you with twelve basketsful left over to share. It is the spiritual discernment that is infinite and multiplies as form. Only God-creation can multiply. Only God-consciousness can multiply and discernment of a spiritual principle is God-consciousness. We are right there with Jesus when we realize a spiritual principle. That is God-consciousness.

All spiritual discernment bypasses intellectual conditioning; we grasp it intuitively and the intuition which is a higher faculty impresses itself immediately on the mind; it bypasses the intellect or, in some cases, it might touch the intellect with pure reason and filter through. But in any case, it is an immediate impression into the mind which is then interpreted by the intellect in a manner in which we can understand. This is the conditioned aspect of the intellect. For instance, if you are asked to draw a picture of a man or woman, if you are Caucasian you would probably draw a picture of a white man or white woman. But if you were Asian you would draw a picture of an Asian man or woman or if you were African you would draw a picture of an African man or woman. That is your conditioned intellect at play. If you were asked to draw your dream house you would probably draw a contemporary version or an American version of whatever your taste might happen to be and it could differ entirely from an Asian or an African citizen because your cultural background is different. This is part of your conditioned intellect.

So when we discern the spiritual principle of supply, we can be sure we are going to experience fulfillment because the form it will take will be according to our conditioned intellect which means fulfillment to us. For instance, if I, understanding the principle of supply, was in need of a home, it would not be a cabin in Timbuktu. It would probably be a beautiful cottage on the beach because that is my idea of a dream home. So that is my conditioned intellect. Okay?

The return based on your realization is usually abundant with your twelve baskets left over to share. But the major thing is, having come to this realization, your faith in this is established and never again will you experience lack. If you have a temporary experience of lack, your faith will be so strong, your conviction will be so great, that you will not fear; you will know, "Oh no, I've got this realization, this is my consciousness, this belongs to me," and more than that, "I am supply. I am a state of consciousness which is realized supply, so I am that." We have to learn to put aside our personal sense, our sense of being a person, and realize I am the Christ-consciousness and to this degree I know the secret of supply. So I am that, and I must stand on that. Standing on that, then, supply has to be formed by the mind and the mind has to be obedient to your decision to stand on it. Always.

You can see now why we had to have the mind work first, because you are not going to be able to grasp the principle of supply or the principle of healing, which is really one and the same, without understanding you have dominion over that mind and what the mind is and why you have dominion over it. Everything functions this way. I am consciousness, the mind is my instrument, and the intellect is my interpreter.

Supply: the Visible Action of the Christ

Now what we have to share from this bounty that comes back to us is the visible action of the individual, of the Christ. When Jesus multiplied the loaves and fishes, he was giving visible proof of his understanding of spiritual supply. If for instance we didn't share our invisible and visible supply, then it would dry up. This is the entire principle. This is the basis of it: I *have*. And whatever I have can only expand and grow as I share. If I don't share it, it dries up.

Now let's look at spiritual supply and the way you miss the boat a lot. Let's take this class okay? For over three weeks, I've been working and keeping my mind filled with truth in preparation for this class, but what was I doing all of these weeks? I have been spiritually supplying my mind with the truth. Over three weeks I constantly, day and night, spiritually supplied my mind, very impersonally, because I wasn't talking to anybody, I wasn't teaching a class; this was inner work, with me as the instrument. I, consciousness, as the creator, the mind as my instrument and the intellect is the interpreter. The language I use, the teaching I teach, that is the intellect. You see? According to my conditioning, according to my culture.

All right, we come to class and what am I doing? Now I am acting on this. I am visibly sharing what has been discerned over these last three weeks. You cannot indulge in that kind of inner activity without your spiritual supply deepening, without it being added to, without it expanding. So everything that is being shared with you today is instantly coming back to me through you as love, respect, attention, tuition, the practical things. Can you see that? It is an instantaneous return. So the visible action is the proof to you that I am an instrument for this work to come through and your response is visible proof to me that it is true. This is my proof that it is true. So I am convinced this principle works. Here is the visible proof: They came back again today [laughter] and I didn't have to lose any sleep.

But my faith is not that strong yet and there is always enough personal sense to make you doubt. The devil's tempter. Always that which once again causes us to go a little deeper, causes us to throw ourselves at the feet of the Christ. And then? The purification. Then a little more light comes through and a little more action takes place. But prayer without action is of no use. It has to be followed by action and that is why we serve.

Stages of Giving

In chapter 11, "Breaking the Bonds of Humanhood" from *Man Was Not Born to Cry,*[*] there is a description of how a student evolves and comes to this point. You can see yourselves from the day you started:

> When a person reaches the point where he comes to spiritual teaching for help, usually he will put forth considerable effort and devotion spending both time and money; but all this effort and devotion, time and money, are being spent for the furthering of his own spiritual progress. In this first stage, he is not thinking in terms of a spiritual way of life; he is not thinking in terms of a world struggling for freedom: he is seeking primarily for something that will meet his own individual needs and, surprisingly enough, sometimes he will not make too much effort, or spend too much money, even in seeking his own welfare. The time does come, even in these first years, however, when he will go to any amount of trouble, give any amount of devotion, or spend any amount of money for the purpose of meeting his needs.
>
> When the student arrives at the second stage, he has already received some measure of healing and harmony, and is beginning to think in terms of others. He tries to interest his friends and relatives in the teaching he has found; he buys books to give them, or in some other way gives something of himself to, and for, others. When that happens, we can be assured that he has entered the path, (but not until that time, until he starts thinking of others, he has not entered the path,) and that he will undoubtedly go deeper and deeper into spiritual consciousness because he is now thinking less in terms of himself, less of his own progress,

---

[*] Joel S. Goldsmith, *Man Was Not Born to Cry* (Longboat Key, FL: Acropolis Books).

less of his personal welfare, and is beginning to share and include others in his concern.

As the entire emphasis shifts from himself to others, however, he is no longer concerned about what he can get from the teaching, or whether it will give him all that he needs. By this time, enough fruitage has appeared in his experience so that it is virtually taken for granted that this is his way. With this attitude, he has entered the third stage, which is an essential stage before he can come into the fullness of spiritual consciousness and experience the fruitage of the added things. This is the place in consciousness where he is beginning to think in terms of the particular message and of how it can help the world. Now his thought centers on how he can give of himself, how he can serve in some way so that others may benefit from this work, and how he can devote himself unselfishly to a spiritual work. There is now not a seeking to draw to himself, but rather a seeking to give of himself, to devote himself to others, a seeking to benefit the world. Rather than permitting his life to be centered on his own welfare, and that of his own family, his horizon is now being broadened to embrace the whole world.

Yes, I Can

Now when this third stage, which is, as he says, essential, before we can come to the full attainment of the Christ, the full attainment of spiritual consciousness, when this stage of giving happens, then you have entered the first degree of Christhood and are yourselves being used as an instrument for the Christ-consciousness. When this third stage is discerned, when we experience this and are now serving in that spirit of not getting but giving of ourselves—giving of ourselves, our time, our money and giving up this world—then we are really practicing the principle of spiritual supply. We are then able to say to the world, "Yes, I in the name of the Christ can help you, yes I in the name of the Christ, can heal you, yes I in the name of the Christ can supply you." And as you adopt that attitude and as you come into the realization of what that means, you can speak for the entire Christhood when you say "Yes I can, in the name of the Christ." You have the absolute totality of the Christhood behind you but not if it is just words. It has to be discerned and so we start where we are and we begin to accept the responsibility for healing work or service.

Do you know that every bit of service that you offer to your spiritual activity has a greater and deeper meaning and effect in consciousness than all of the accomplishments you could make in the outer world? Every time you come into a class-room or a study center or any group activity with the purpose of joining your companions on the path to be of service, every time you take a tablecloth home and wash it, or dust the fur-niture in this study center, this has more effect in human consciousness than if you built the Empire State Building, because this is discernment, this is doing the humble things for the greater glory of God. This is humility pouring through the individual.

There are students who don't enter the center without putting money in the bowl as an action after prayer. Prayer and then action. Now nobody looks to see who is doing it. It is nobody's business. But the Father who "seeth in secret, rewardeth openly." All these years, and many of you can testify to this, all of these years that you have been in this work you have watched your lives change, you have watched prosperity come into your lives, you have watched your careers grow and expand, you have received the respect and the accolades from your peers in business, in the arts, in the professions—you've seen all of that. Do you think it is something you have done?

If you do, you might lose it. It is not what you have done, it is what you *are*. It is what you are that is drawing to itself this visible truth of the principle realized in your consciousness; as you have cast your bread in the recognition of the Christ of your co-workers and your friends and your business associates, then this is the bread that has come back to you. Do you see that?

"It is in this third stage," Joel says, "that we notice the miracle that has taken place in our lives; life has ceased to be a struggle, and the added things come pouring in upon us, not by taking thought, not by trying to demonstrate them, but as the reflex action of the givingness of ourselves." It is ourselves that have to be given away. Ourselves. The only bread that we can have and the only bread that will come back to us is the bread that we cast on the waters. What we do not give out cannot possibly come back. What we do give out cannot fail to return to us. And no one can touch it without burning their fingers. We are the life of God in individual expression embodying everything necessary for our experience. It is much like an individual seed which contains within itself everything necessary for its unfoldment and development into a full-grown tree bearing fruit.

Activity of Consciousness

So it is with us. Our good appears to come to us through these outside activities: a business, a profession, or even through some other person. But even though we seem to be drawing our supply from these sources, nevertheless it cannot come to us unless we set in motion the activity of consciousness within ourselves that draws back to us that which is already our own. Continuing in "Breaking the Bonds of Humanhood":

In this third stage of spiritual unfoldment, we learn that our participation in this spiritual activity and our desire to contribute to the betterment of mankind, and to be active in some service that is to benefit others are the putting out the bread that is to return to us and it is of a permanent nature. This is the truth which every mystic has known: The secret is giving, not getting; outpouring not withholding; selflessness, not selfishness. It is only in proportion to the outpouring of ourselves, to our dedication and service to others, and to what we give that the return can come to us.

Now of course you understand that principle, the basic principle, is oneness. The reason it has to return to us is because we are only giving it to ourselves. Never make the mistake of thinking you are serving the world or serving the public or serving students; you are only serving yourself; the appearance is you are serving others. But if you have the discernment of the principle, as Joel used to say, he wasn't pious, he was smart. He said, "I know what I'm doing. I'm doing this for myself, I'm not doing this for you." It is very easy to fall into the belief that you are helping others, but if you are high enough in spiritual consciousness, you realize there is no one to be helped. And so you are being given the opportunity to help yourself through service, through sharing, through giving.

Depending on where we are in consciousness, we give material things, and with deepening, we give spiritually. It just depends on the degree of consciousness that a person has attained or the degree of Christ-consciousness. The work that has been done by The Infinite Way and other spiritual teachings over the last hundred years has seemingly caused humanity to evolve into a world which is now conscious of the rights of other human beings. That is a major step forward. But that is not going to eliminate wars; it is not going to

SPIRITUAL HEALING, SPIRITUAL SUPPLY   113

eliminate violence or greed or crime. As long as there is any human consciousness left to cater to that kind of thing, it is going to manifest. And we as spiritual students who know the principle at whatever degree our knowledge is must begin to realize this for the world.

Serving the World

For instance, in doing world work, let us be the instrument of spiritual supply to realize that which we are looking at. In my case, what came to me on the subject of violence and the wars in Bosnia and Rwanda was that this was error turning back on itself. This was error destroying itself. This then goes into the mind and is impressed on the mind, and since it is a degree of truth, not the highest, (I'm sure there are higher degrees of truth than that which came through me) but it satisfied me at the moment, do you see? That is what the intellect does for you, it satisfies you at the moment. So that goes into the mind.

Now when we do this kind of work, we don't think of it as a service to humankind; we are looking for answers for ourselves primarily. And in the final analysis, that is who it helps. It is my consciousness that perceives this and so I'm the one who needs it, and then the mind being the illuminator, the reflector, reflects it back to me.

Look at what is happening in the Middle East after so many years of spiritual work manifesting in the outer work of the principles. The Peace Prize was awarded this year and look at the carnal mind trying to destroy it. See? But that is a service; Mr. Carter is the visible principle here. He is the visible proof of the inner work that has been done. What you are is shouted from the housetops and we can look around and see the visible proof of your Christ-consciousness in your communities; it is there in hundreds of ways.

Students miss many opportunities to serve. I have witnessed the grace of God being rejected by students. Grace is your discernment, your spiritual discernment, and it appears as the visible forms. Opportunities to serve are given to us, I'm sure, by the hundreds every day and we are blind to these opportunities. Ideas flow into our minds that we don't act on. We file them away for future use; we procrastinate. We say, "This is a good idea and I'll get back to it," and we fool around and delay it until the life has gone out of it or somebody else picks it up. We lose our opportunity to be of service.

And those of us who do that, what are we blocked by? The intellect. "Well, I can't do this now because . . ." "This isn't right because . . ." "This isn't logical . . . the time isn't right." The intellect can give you a million excuses why this idea should not come into manifestation. Then there is mental inertia which is the biggest problem of human beings. We just don't want to get down to work. The word "work" sends us climbing the walls. Nobody wants to work. But this path is *a* work. The greatest work with the greatest rewards. I have seen students bring beautiful creative ideas into consciousness and just pass them on to somebody else or abrogate their spiritual responsibility completely and it goes in the wastecan. I have seen students given opportunities to serve in their spiritual activity; they will take on responsibilities and then pass them on to somebody else or abrogate them. This happens. It happens right here, right here in this group. Hundreds of wasted opportunities.

But as I said earlier, those small services are more essential to your ongoing and more important as they enter human consciousness than if you built the Empire State Building.

What, then, causes us to think this way? The intellect: the conditioned, conceptualized intellect. We think of glory, we think of titles, huge salaries, gorgeous homes, and the accolades of business and professions. "The respect of our peers." And if that is where we place ourselves, then that of course is what we get. But only in limited fashion.

The Whole Garment

When you go for supply, don't go for money. When you go for the principle of spiritual supply, go for the whole garment. If you go for money, you might get money and lose your health. And if you go for health, you might lose your income. Why split it? The Christ encompasses all. Let's have it all. Let's go for the whole garment. Let's go for the Christ-consciousness. Let's not be stingy. But the stickler is, we have to be the instrument and until we grow up, until we grow into that adult spiritual consciousness, we will just be holding out our hands for a bit of candy here and there.

Now it is obvious, since we are talking about proof or conviction, it is obvious that as I have shared my spiritual discernment with you, and as others have shared their spiritual discernment with you, that I am being fed, I am being clothed, I am being housed, and the more I share, the more I have to share. The more responsive you are, the greater is your depth for receiving, and the more you share, the greater is your depth for receiving. As I share with you, I'm leaving room to receive more, but if I block it up, if I withhold, then it is to my own detriment.

If I withhold, you sit there, and you look at me and you wait and maybe because I don't care for the color of your clothes today, or don't care for your lifestyle, I'm not going to

give you what I've got. I'm going to pass judgment on you and
so I'm not going to share. Now look at what I've done. Who
is going to be hurt in this, you or me? You are not going to be
hurt. You might suffer a little temporary lack of whatever I
had but if that is what you need, it will appear in the form of
another teacher. I'm the one who will be hurt because I will
have lost my opportunity to demonstrate and express spiritual
supply. I would have turned my back on my opportunity to
serve because perhaps I had a human dislike of you or maybe
because you are not behaving the way I think you should. So
you are not hurt by that; I'm the one who is hurt. If we cannot
love one another, how in the world are we going to love God?
If we cannot serve one another, we cannot serve God because
God is served through service to humankind.

So you can see that the spiritual discernment of the
principle is where your permanent supply is, because then
it becomes you. You can then say with Jesus, "I am supply."
When you have that principle realized in your consciousness,
you can say "I am supply" and there is no end to it. "Ask and
ye shall receive." I have. Pour. Multiply. I can do all things
through Christ and why is that? Because I have attained the
Christ-consciousness. My consciousness is my infinite supply.
Joel says, "That which I am seeking, I already am." So if I am
seeking supply of any nature, I'm usually seeking amiss, and I
am praying amiss, because the principle is revealed within my
Self. It is not revealed by man whose breath is in his nostrils.
But it is expressed visibly according to my conditioned intellect as fulfillment.

I always like to hear Joel quote Joan of Arc. When she was
asked "In what language does God speak to you?" she said,
"I don't know in which language God speaks, but I hear him
in French." So I hear God in English and you hear God in

English because of our conditioned intellect. If we heard him in German, it would not be a fulfillment. Do you see?

The work that each student undertakes in preparation for these classes and these workshops and the care of the Study Center, all of this is the manifesting of spiritual supply flowing through them. The effort that each one of you lovely people take to come such far distances and arrange your lives to accommodate an entire week of classwork, this is your spiritual supply; this is it. You are expressing it, don't you see? *I* have, *I* am; you are here, you are doing it, you are acting on that. And so, *I* am supply. You can realize that. *I* am demonstrating it. And it is infinite. It is infinite because it is not personal to me or to you. It is the light in My consciousness. *I* am come in you that you might have life and have it abundantly. *I* the Christ am come in you. And if we can accept that, the glory of God is made manifest on earth as it is in heaven.

Let us close for our noonday meditation.

Spiritual Healing, Spiritual Supply (continued)

Grace Operating in Our Consciousness

NOW AS WE ARE called upon to do the healing work of any nature, for any claim, whether for our families, our friends, our business associates, or the world, we rely on the consciousness of truth, the awareness of that invisible Presence and Power. The flow of peace, the flow of a sense of baptism, of water, even the experience of intense fire, all of these are evidences of things unseen; these are symbols or signs of grace operating in our consciousness. This is also identified as the descent of the Holy Ghost, the spirit of the Lord upon us which is the Illuminator reflecting back to us the Truth of being; this is the Knowing, the Consciousness, the Wisdom, the eternal Truth, that which knows, the Illumination. And this is shared as we experience it in our consciousness whether alone or as a group as we just did; this goes into human consciousness and it constitutes your spiritual supply and mine.

Every time I go into meditation for anyone who has called for help, then I am an instrument through which My spiritual supply—My, capital M, My—is flowing into the consciousness of humankind and because I am the instrument of that, I am that. Bearing in mind now I am consciousness, we must rise above the sense of being a person, even an individual. We are impersonal consciousness individualized. I am; I am that. I am that *I Am*. It is an impersonal state of consciousness. Then as that spiritual supply flows through us in the form of healings or creative endeavors or family relationships or business, however it takes form, that is the evidence of your spiritual supply which is your consciousness of the principle of supply. Your spiritual supply is the consciousness of the principle of supply and I am that. As I am aware of that, I am that *I Am*.

So before we went into meditation,[*] this group of claims was presented to us and each one of those claims indicate a lack of spiritual wisdom, a lack of spiritual consciousness. In a couple of cases, there were lists of "I lack this, I lack this, I lack this." There is only one lack, because everything that the student seems to lack is an image or a concept of spiritual supply. Now to go back to the first part of our practice of this principle: We cannot lack anything; to say I lack is an outright lie. I do not lack anything. If I lack money, I give all I have at the moment. If I lack companionship, I find someone to companion with. Even if it is a kitten or a bird I am companioning, therefore my companionship must return to me. If I lack love, I must give it. If I have inharmonious relationships, then I must become harmony personified. I must forgive "seventy times seven." That is an unlimited spiritual supply and nobody can forgive for you. As we forgive, we are forgiven. As we supply, we are supplied. As we love, we are loved. As we companion, we are companioned with.

---

[*] A group of written claims were submitted in preparation for this class session.

It is a principle. It is as simple as that. That is absolute spiritual law and that's where we start. Sharing the material evidence of spiritual grace is where we start. Then, as we see that principle in operation, we are practicing the Presence and we are ready to go higher as was explained in the first half of this class. We are ready now to discern the reality, to become the principle itself in action. And in order to do and be that, we have to experience it as an act of consciousness. "That which I am seeking, I am."

Disciplines are Necessary

Now that shouldn't be too hard for you to grasp. Any density is a reluctance to grasp it because the responsibility is overwhelming for a human being. Human beings just do not want to take this responsibility, but you are past the stage of being a human being and this is your next step in Christhood. That is why you are here; you cannot avoid it. Are you aware that this is your answer to all of those claims you put in the basket? Disciplines which you don't want to practice are absolutely necessary. Fear has to be dissolved through courage, through faith. These have to be drawn from your own inner resources with no outlining as to how grace is to appear.

Some students feel that supply should be present before any decision is made. "Well if I get the money, I'll go to that class" or "If I can save up enough I might be able to take that vacation." Or "If a new job comes through, I might be able to lend you some money or go to college" or something like that, instead of taking dominion. Making the decision, "Yes, I will. Yes, I can."

Now if you understand what we have been talking about since yesterday morning, you will have to realize and stand on this principle and not waver. If you vacillate, that is just the kind of picture you are going to get. "I have, I will, I am." You see, whatever your decision, the mind has to comply. It has to comply. But if you let reason come into it and logic and doubt come into it from the direction of the intellect which is reminding you this has never been done before, or how do you know you can do this, how are you ever going to know you can do this until you do it? And this is what I mean when I say you are at a place where nobody can do it for you anymore. You've got to take this next step and stumble and fall, but you will get up again. We've all stumbled. Nobody achieves one hundred percent.

If you wait for what you need before you make a decision, you are putting the cart before the horse spiritually. The last class that I attended of Joel's was the last class he gave in the United States. At that time, I had no money, a husband who was adamantly opposed to this work, and two children, a baby and a young teenager that I would have to leave to go to Chicago to that class. I was in a real turmoil until Joel wrote me and said, "I shall look forward to seeing you in Chicago." Now that was a command to me. I wrestled with what is my will and what is thy will; do I have the right to leave my children with a husband who is so adamantly opposed? Do I have the right to go without his permission, God help me I should have to have permission to go? Do I have the right to take this money which would be like taking food out of the mouths of my children and do this? I was dying; I was being crucified. Then as I was pondering all this in such misery, I was told I no longer had a will of my own and I no longer had a mind of my own and that was the healing. All I had to do was make the decision.

When I did, the money came two days before I was to leave from the most unexpected source. My father had had a life insurance policy in my name and had forgotten all about it. It had a small cash value and he cashed it in and sent it to me and that covered my trip to Chicago. That's all. It covered my trip to Chicago so that I did not have to take any money from my husband.

Standing on Principle

Here, then, is faith that becomes courage. You stand on the principle: it is either true or it is not. If it is not, then I'm wasting my time and my life and if it is true, then I have eternity and conscious union with God. I have illumination; I have the evidence of things unseen. And so you stand or you fall. There is no in between. On the basis of my conviction that this was reality, this was real, and that the anti-Christ was an illusion, I went to Chicago. Can you imagine how I would have felt and how much I would have lost, how much you would have lost, had I not attended that last class in Chicago?

My children were fine, my husband was irate, but that didn't seem to matter. What is at work is division. In scripture we hear "Jesus lifted his eyes to heaven and turned to the disciples and said, 'Break.'" And they broke the loaves of bread and the fishes and fed ten thousand people. Then elsewhere he lifted his eyes to heaven and said, "Lazarus, come forth." And then on the cross it was written "He lifted his eyes to heaven and he said, 'It is finished.'"

Now I interpret that to mean we lift our inner vision to the highest level we can reach and that is our spiritual integrity and when that level is reached, we stand on it. If we don't stand on it, then we have to go back down a step. You see, every time we successfully stand on the level of our spiritual integrity, we fill out there for a while. Then we are ready for the next step and each step is more difficult than the one before. Had I given in to my human feelings in May of 1964, there would be no me talking to you today. Now that might not seem like a lot to other people, but it's my whole life. That is spiritual perception, spiritual healing, and it is standing on the principle. We have opportunities all the time to honor our spiritual integrity and to stand on the principles as we know them. This is what makes us healers when we succeed.

There was another time when I was able to stand on the principles. Some of you have heard this story before: In about my second year of study, I found I had a lump under my right arm and it was painful. After twenty-four hours, it became more painful and a red streak began to run down my upper arm in the muscle. I was working every day with Joel at the time and on this particular morning when my daughter got off to school and my husband went to work and my young son was still asleep, I just looked at it. I was sitting at the breakfast table and something came over me, just like a great strength rising up in me and as I looked at it I thought, "Okay. Let's just see how much power you've got. If you can kill me, go ahead, let's see it." Then I forgot about it; I went on about my work in the house, tending to my son, and then didn't look at it again until some hours later, I looked, and it was gone. The swelling was gone, the pain was gone, just a faint reminder of a red streak. Now that is standing on the principle. Once again, "Either this is true, or it is not true, and I need to know." Your telling me this is true is not going to make it true for me. I can believe you have this wonderful thing, but it doesn't belong to me until I experience it.

There are times when we think we are surrendering to God's will for us or we are taking over dominion of our life and believe me it is God's will that we take dominion over our life; that is why God gave it to us. As a matter of fact, since it belongs to us, I don't think God *can* take it back. I know that's what I was told many years ago that I had reached a state of consciousness where I had to begin to teach; I knew that my entire human concept of family and everyday living would have to be dissolved if I entered teaching; I asked that this cup pass from me and as you heard me say before, I was told, "Even God cannot take away from you what belongs to you by right of consciousness." That was the night of my ordination.

Not even God can take away from you what belongs to you by right of consciousness; dominion we are told, is ours. All we have to do is accept it. So even if we make a decision to step out on this and say "I will do this thing," and even if we expect the grace of God will provide this since we are standing on the principle, there is still that perversity in human consciousness that will outline how the grace of God is going to provide this for us. Then we may miss the opportunity because we are so busy with our concepts of how this is going to appear to us that we don't see what is already before us.

We may have our eyesight on a vacation to Europe and someone sends us an airline ticket to Hawaii and we say, "Well, no, I've got my heart set on Europe and so I'm sorry I can't accept your free ticket to Hawaii." Remember when Joel received the cablegram from Hawaii when he was in San Francisco? A small group of people had read his book *The Infinite Way* which he'd had published himself and in the wire they asked, "When are you coming to Hawaii?" He wired back, "I'm on my way." That, of course, was his next step.

In the case of this free trip to Hawaii, as opposed to me paying for a trip to Europe, then I must look at this and ask "There is something here that I don't consciously perceive, but God constitutes my being." Then I would think that this is an indication that there is something I'm to be doing in Hawaii.

So let's not outline how grace is to come to us and let us be very alert. The trip to Hawaii *is* the grace of God.

Everything should be translated into the presence, power, and intelligence of God, and obedience to the assignment given, such as, going to Hawaii instead of Europe. Be obedient to that, be quick to perceive that this is of God not of man, be quick to realize that this is not outlining, this is the Presence, this is the grace of God. Begin to perceive the bigger picture and not merely want what you consider your problems be taken from you. See them as opportunities presented to you to stand on the principle.

The Entire Christhood

I said to you earlier that I could accept a claim for the entire Christhood and you could do this too, in the name of *I*; I can accept the responsibility for the entire Christhood for healing and teaching of a spiritual nature. "Whatsoever ye shall ask in my name in the name of *I*." In our work, we have a beautiful practitioners' group of seven and they can accept a claim for the entire group. Anyone in the group you could call with the absolute knowledge that the entire group healing consciousness is there to handle it. And so by the same token, you, as you grow in your awareness of the fulness of the Christ-consciousness, can also realize "I am accepting this claim for the entire Christhood and so all I have to do is be still and let it do the work." It performeth that which is appointed for me; my part is to accept and then be still. But I've got to have that inner experience; I've got to have that spiritual supply come through.

In Chapter 7 in *Man Was Not Born to Cry*, Joel says, "What you accept for yourself, you must accept for every other person because there is only one I. So if someone says he is ill, and you know that you are not, you do not have to accept that and you do not have to reject it." Now isn't that plain enough?

There is one *I*. There is one *I* and if you come to me with a claim of cancer or a prostate problem; I know I don't have a prostate problem, right? It is easier for me to realize that you don't have one either even if you are a man. But if you come to me with a claim of breast cancer, then that is more difficult because I am a woman and all of those concepts of being a woman are in the intellect, so it becomes more difficult to realize that I don't have that.

But if I can rise high enough above the state of womanhood, or femininity or femaleness, and see clearly "well I don't have that," then I can speak for all womankind. Do you see how this gets out of the realm of individual healing to world work? But you the practitioner have to know this. You have to realize that this is a female claim or this is a male claim; it has nothing to do with spiritual being at all. Then if I can rise into my spiritual *I*-ness, my spiritual identity, then I know I don't have this and since I am One, then it is not possible that you would have it either.

Now this is a little more difficult state to rise to and you cannot do it every time, but as you practice, you will reach these heights from time to time and healing is instantaneous, depending of course on your patient. There are patients who respond and patients who do not. Too, practitioners are not in the same high state of consciousness 24 hours a day. So each time you go within to do what we call healing work, you will have a different experience. If you expect there to be a formula, if you expect the same thing to happen every time, then you will be missing the boat because each experience is unique. Especially if you do the deeper work, where you understand that this is not just for this individual, there is a wider, broader connotation here. And as your work deepens, the more claims that you handle, the more time that you have to work on the inner plane rather than the outer plane, the deeper your consciousness and understanding of these principles grows. Eventually you get to the place where you realize that any claim can be met but they are not all met. But with God nothing is impossible, nothing. It is just that we have not risen to that state of consciousness yet where some claims can be broken. There are some claims in human consciousness that are more difficult than others.

You can speak for all humanity, just as you can speak for the entire Christhood, when you understand *I*, when you have that conviction behind it, and you won't have the conviction until you stand on the principle; the conviction comes with the proof, the evidence of things unseen. Our spiritual supply is not dependent on us. In the analogy of the branch to the tree, wouldn't it be silly to cut ourselves off and expect ourselves to be supplied eternally? To cut ourselves off from the trunk of the tree and expect that we could infinitely provide for ourselves? The life comes up through the trunk of the tree.

Healing Work

When we do healing work, we turn as a branch in the tree inwardly to the trunk and we realize that our life, our juices, our sap, flows from the roots up from the trunk of the tree to the branch. If one branch turns to us and says, "Will you give me some help, I don't have too many leaves growing on my branch," what would one limb think of another? Wouldn't she say, "Well, all you have to do is draw it forth from the trunk." That is sharing, that is knowing the truth. Now if the limb who has asked for help forgets and comes back and says, "Well, my leaves all fell off, what do I do now?" the other branch says, "Stand on the principle. Go back to the principle. Draw from the trunk of the tree, draw from the roots." And the limb that has asked for help says, "I forgot. I forgot. Can you help me out one more time?" The limb above her, in this case the practitioner, again draws from the root, draws from the trunk, and it comes up and goes into the limb that has no leaves. And once again, the limb is fruitful and has leaves with blossoms on it.

Now that is similar to the way we are. Whenever you are called upon for healing work, don't panic, and don't be afraid that you are responsible, that there is something that you have got to do. All you have to remember is the trunk. As Joel says in *I Am the Vine*,* "Thank God for that trunk!" All we have to do is go within and draw on that inner resource and understand that since we are one, it is drawn through our consciousness, because we have asked for it. Now that is a healing principle.

There are some inspirational examples I would like to share with you. One story is of a mother and a child: The mother was a practitioner of metaphysics and the little child had the measles and she sat up all night with the little boy nursing him through his illness and doing her spiritual work. Toward morning she felt "Well that's the best I can do," so she went downstairs and was making breakfast when the little boy came down, dressed, but he still had all of the evidence of measles over his body, splotches and a temperature. He sat down, ate his breakfast, and then got up to go to the coat closet to get his coat to go outdoors. It was midwinter with a foot of snow on the ground and his mother looked at this little boy with all those splotches and the temperature and she stood there and she heard, "Choose ye." She stood very quietly. The little boy put his coat on, went outside, danced in

---

* Joel S. Goldsmith, *I Am the Vine* (Longboat Key, FL : Acropolis Books).

the snow, jumped in the snow for hours. When he came back in a couple of hours later all the blotches were gone and the fever was gone.

Of course, that is very difficult to do. I had similar experiences when my son was little and in a nursery school. I think it was over a period of five days that he caught every conceivable childhood disease there was, even scarlet fever and that was the last one. My daughter and I watched that. It got to be funny. The measles would fade and the chicken pox would break out, one thing after another. And within a period of four or five days, he went through the entire gamut of childhood diseases without any supervision by a doctor and no medication by standing on the principle. I had a friend who used to say "Boy you sure are brave, I'd be too terrified to do that with my children," but it was a conviction, an inner knowing that this had to be truth. It had to be truth, but I didn't know it until it was proven in my consciousness.

There is another story of a farmer who had a hernia for a couple of years which was causing him a great deal of pain. He was farming every day and driving heavy equipment. One day, it got to be too much for him and he thought, "I just can't go on any longer with this," and so he got off his tractor and went to lean on a tree and as he stood there, he heard a voice that said, "This is not going to get any better; you might as well go and have surgery done." With that he reared back and said, "I would rather die first." He got back on his tractor again and a couple of hours later he realized all the pain was gone and the hernia was healed. Now that is conviction.

Bear in mind now, all of these trials are mental images. There never is anything wrong to begin with. These are beliefs imposed on your body, beliefs which have been accepted into your consciousness and of course your mind has to be obedient to your consciousness, so it imposes them on your body. But the same consciousness that put them there can awaken and dissolve them. The mind cannot do anything about them. The mind has no power, remember. So you and I can reject them, dissolve them; you cannot heal them because there is nothing to heal. They are just images in thought.

There is another story, which is a favorite of mine, of a practitioner who was called to the home of a dying man who was in the last throes of lymphoma. She had been reading that afternoon about the perfection of spiritual man and the completeness and beauty of spiritual man and it was very clear in her consciousness the reality of spiritual man. When she walked into this man's bedroom—she'd never seen him before—she sat down in a chair next to his bed; he was lying with his mouth open and his eyes closed and seeming to breathe his last and as she looked at him, inwardly she began to chuckle. She was thinking, "Boy he sure doesn't look like any perfect spiritual man to me, not really my idea of a perfect spiritual man." And she just looked at him inwardly chuckling. She was thinking to herself, "This is a joke." Suddenly, he began to smile; the corners of his mouth turned up a little bit and then presently he opened his eyes and he smiled more broadly and then all of a sudden, he burst out laughing and she did too. In a few minutes he put his hand on hers and he said, "Do you think I might be able to get up?"

Do you see? That is a classic example of knowing the truth, but not knowing it with your mind, not knowing it with your intellect, but realizing what a joke it is to think of God in that condition. And this was so clear in that practitioner's mind that all she could do was laugh. And of course, there was a time that Joel was attending a man at a Christian Science hospital and he had promised some little children to take them to the movies. Just as he was to go pick the children up, the nurse at the hospital called and said, "Mr. so and so is on his last legs, I think you'd better come." Joel thanked her and as he hung up the phone he said, "Oh I hate to disappoint those children, I promised them I'd take them to see that movie. That man is not going to die until I get back," so he took the children to the movie and sure enough, when he came back the man was still alive.

So you can see that if you know the truth, that the truth can set you free as well as others who come to you. This is what we call spiritual healing. Actually, no healing is accomplished. It is a bringing to the light the truth of being.

Faith is conviction because you *know*. If you are frightened or doubtful, just ask that you be imbued with faith. "Give me faith to stand on this, give me conviction to stand on this." Whatsoever ye ask in my name, whatsoever is of the quality of God, you can ask for. But you cannot ask for a healing of something that doesn't exist. You cannot ask for supply when it is omnipresent and you are the source of it. You cannot ask for what you already have. Faith is not a quality of the intellect, so you cannot expect the intellect to provide it. The intellect provides reasons and it provides reasons why you can't. But faith is a state of spiritual consciousness, not human consciousness, and it is evidenced by our conviction that allows us to stand on these principles.

The Experience

In the essay, *The Deep Silence of My Peace,*[*] we are told to turn away from the picture, turn away from our mind, and turn within to that deep pool of our being. This is the healing

---

[*] Joel S. Goldsmith, *The Deep Silence of My Peace* (Longboat Key, FL: Acropolis Books).

principle which is beyond words and thoughts. When we do
this, and it is a beautiful principle, a beautiful experience,
and as we wait for that feeling of peace, we drop the claim;
we drop the person, we release everything outside the door
of our consciousness and turn within to that deep pool and
we receive the grace which is evidenced in innumerable ways.
With me it is usually a flooding of my consciousness with
peace, sometimes a tremendous breath, a release. Joel used
to call it a "click" when he knew God was on the field, but I've
never had that particular experience. Usually with me it is
what I've just described or the feeling of an invisible Presence
that seems to surround me or is embracing me or sometimes
is as if it enters me. It is invisible, but it's a tangible substance.

But this peace, this deep peace that comes, floods you,
it invades your entire consciousness. Or at times it can be a
light. I've had experiences where the entire room was filled
with light, where it just stopped short behind my eyes and
suddenly it grows and grows and grows and I'm aware that
the entire room is lit with my eyes closed. Other times it can
be something as simple as what we just did. Catching your
breath. It's different and unique to everyone, but it is a healing
principle that is beyond words and thoughts.

Of course, there are times when we cannot reach that state
of consciousness immediately. And then we use the letter of
truth to lift the I up out of the intellect. We know the truth,
but we are knowing the truth with our intellect. You can call
this contemplative meditation. Sometimes you can read a
chapter in a book or a paragraph in a book or open the Bible or
many times you can open a book and you'll find exactly what
you are looking for. But you are not going to find any truth
in a book that is going to do the healing. You are not going to
find anything outside of your consciousness that is going to
do the healing. That truth that you read about might inspire

you to go within and touch the center of your being and the contemplative meditation that you are having might lift you to where you can make this inner contact but none of that has any power. Your words have no power. The words you speak and the words you read have no power until they are touched by Grace. When you have that release you can be assured that the grace of God is upon you, the spirit of the Lord, the Law, is upon you. You know that, you feel that, you are experiencing that, and you are convinced of that. Nobody can tell you any different. And that is where your faith comes in, when you have that experience.

By thy grace we are healed. "Thy grace is my sufficiency." So it is "thy grace" we are looking for. It is the healing, the redeeming action, not words, not thoughts.

Well thank you so much.

Questions and Answers

G OOD EVENING. Well this is the third day of our closed classwork and our sixth session together. I think it is time we pause for some questions and clarification on what we have had so far, and after we are through with the written ones, if we have time, please raise your hand and we will take care of them tonight.

Q: Our first question is: *Dominion versus self-will. How do we know which is which?*

A: This question comes up every now and then, which indicates to me a fear of making a mistake or committing an erroneous decision or committing an erroneous act. What we should realize here is that biblically speaking, we are told to "choose ye this day whom we will serve." Now the very fact that we are told to choose ye, means you choose whom you will serve, which indicates to me that free will is involved. I am to choose. Nobody is to choose for me. You are to choose. Nobody is to choose for you so you must have a will with which to choose.

In the human scene remember that everything is the opposite of the spiritual reality and human beings think and believe, that they are beings separate and apart from God. Now what a person considers their free will is as erroneous as their belief of it. There is only one Presence, one Being, and therefore, one Will, one Mind, one Soul, once again appearing as many. So as in the case of the decision which I talked about in yesterday's session, about going to Chicago for Joel's final class in the United States, I thought I had a decision to make. In reality, I was torn apart between my intellectual concept of what I should do as a good human being and my inner spiritual impetus, which was where my will was focused. The dilemma I was in was in "choosing ye." When in my confusion I delivered what I thought my free will was, I was told I no longer had a will of my own and I no longer had a mind of my own. Well of course I never did, but that was the way it came to me that was satisfactory. It was a release that I no longer had any say-so about it and my higher consciousness was prevailing.

Now when we are in a dilemma and the Spirit is pointing one way and the human good is pointing another way, spiritual discernment enters in to show us which is a higher way. Very often we cannot take that higher way and very often we have to be honest with ourselves and say "Well, suffer it to be so now." Sometimes when we have been ill for a while and we can't rise to a spiritual healing, we will have to undergo surgery or medical treatment and while we certainly don't want to do that, we say "Suffer it to be so now." No one is going to be excommunicated for going down a step. In fact, I think it is a little foolish to permit oneself to be nonfunctioning in order to heal a minor physical claim. Too, just like taking a step down and surrendering one's so called will-power which gets us into trouble, often people have beautiful experiences while undergoing surgery or while being treated by a medical physician. After all, if God is not present in the operating room, is not present in the doctor's office, then it is not present anywhere. So spiritual pride quite often can enter into a case like that.

Now this question of dominion is important because along the way, we are told emphatically that in order to unfold spiritually we must assume dominion over our lives. Three years ago, we had a class on dominion—I think it was probably the first or second workshop we had—which I feel is a classic on the subject.* What was brought out in that class is that we have to regain the dominion we had lost as we have followed along like sheep in the beliefs of human consciousness, in the beliefs that are still in our conditioned intellects.

We have to re-take that dominion by standing on our spiritual principle to the best of our ability and by permitting nothing to enter our consciousness of an alien nature to that which we know is spiritual truth. This requires a lot of hard work and for this purpose we are given the disciplines throughout The Infinite Way, especially in the early books, as well as the monthly *Letters* from 1954-1959.** These are the disciplines of clearing our mind in the morning and making our contact with the Source, with the fourth-dimension, dedicating our day to that service and then a couple of hours later doing the same thing all through the day. And of course, a major point few people like to do, which is certainly important, is closing our mind at night before we go to sleep.

Now in assuming dominion with the work we've had on the mind this week, you now know the mind is yours. It is *your* mind and you have dominion over it. But in the past, for

---

* Refer to Recording 194A: January 1992 – "Take Back Dominion". Available for purchase from www.joelgoldsmith.com.

** The 1955 through 1959 *Letters* are compiled in *The Heart of Mysticism* series, (Longboat Key, FL : Acropolis Books).

heaven knows how many thousands of years, we have allowed the mind to run amok and this is why the intellect keeps re-working the same old ideas and the same old forms and why, as we said day before yesterday, history keeps repeating itself, even in our own lives. Even in this single incarnation, you can look back over your life and see, for instance, the same types of people appearing over and over in your life or the same types of experiences. And if you leave your environment to go elsewhere, if you are perceptive, you see the same types of people surrounding you. So what does this tell us? It is my own consciousness and I can't get away from it.

We get married, we get divorced, and then we go out and marry somebody new who looks different and acts different, but it doesn't take us long to discover "This is the same old deal." So whose consciousness is this? This, then, is what we have to take dominion over. We take dominion over the mind and fill it with spiritual truth. We reclaim the intellect and it requires the use of these disciplines. That is practicing the presence of God.

Now once that has been accomplished and the Spirit takes over after you have done all of this work, then you give up dominion. But until you have regained it, you don't have anything to surrender. We can say "Here I am Father, thy will be done, I give you my dominion, I surrender my dominion." You cannot surrender what you do not have, so this is, in the visible world, the process that we go through in our spiritual unfoldment.

We work, work, work for six days and on the seventh day we rest and that is when the Spirit takes over. At that point, you learn that you do not have to be concerned about your self-will because you never had one to begin with. You can see this in a story of Joseph and his brothers in Joel's *Spiritual*

Interpretation of Scripture.[*] In a very high prayer, Joseph says to his brothers, "It was not ye who sent me forward, it was God." This was his acknowledgement that God was all there is. We seem to be going through these trials and tribulations and then we feel we are in error or we feel the carnal mind is functioning through us, or whatever term we want to call it. In reality, and we have had this throughout our work on translation, we translate everything into the presence, power, and activity of God. Then we are really honest and really humble and we see, "Oh my goodness, it was God who sent me here, who sent the lessons I had to learn through this, which I could not have learned in any other way."

It is our resistance, of course, that creates the pain; the human side of us which is called the antichrist resists the Christ. That is why as our I is raised up in consciousness we are told, "Get out of the way. This is a battle between the flesh and the Spirit; let the Spirit do the work." So that is why we keep surrendering. This is what you do when you reach a high enough consciousness in healing work and you can relax in this. *You* don't do any work. The Spirit does the work, the Christ does the work; you and I couldn't heal a broken toenail. As I explained to you yesterday when I had my first experiences with the healing work, it was quite apparent to me that healings were produced and I wasn't intelligent enough to have brought them forth: I didn't know that much. But having had those healings happen, and needing to have a background of metaphysical principles, I had to study the letter of truth. As a matter of fact, Joel told me that I would have to go back and study even Christian Science and Unity, to read some of

---

[*] Joel S. Goldsmith, *Spiritual Interpretation of Scripture* (Camarillo, CA : DeVorss Publications).

that work, so that I would know the difference between The Infinite Way and other metaphysical movements. He indicated I would teach it one day and would have to know the difference.

So dominion versus self-will, how do we know? Just relax. Let the Spirit guide you in that but remember: "Choose ye." You have that power that is a God-given power within you. You have the power of dominion over your life and you can do anything you have a heart's desire to do, because you don't have the power to create a heart's desire in the first place. I mean it. Every thought you think, you think you *can* think, you cannot. You think you can be bad or good but you cannot. These are all beliefs that are imposed upon you in your conditioning. The conditioned intellect keeps saying to you "No, no, no that is a baddie, that is a no-no." Well who told you that? Who said so? Did God tell you that? Your inner spiritual integrity is what you base your dominion on, not what anyone else tells you, not what anyone else tries to get you to do. Always go within and ask, "Now what do I *want* to do?" and then be willing to listen. And it might speak or it might show you. We always have to be intensely alert to our responses from the within, because as we know, they never come in the same way.

Q: *Will you speak more about redemption. How, if at all, does it go beyond forgiving seventy times seven?*

A: Well redemption of course is handled by loving and forgiving. Now the redemption in the context in which we spoke of it this week is a redeeming of those facets of your consciousness you find unpleasant and unable to live with and not wanting in your world anymore. And with spiritual wisdom, we can recognize, "Well this is not a person I'm looking at, this is not a person I'm judging; this is the facet of my own consciousness. I'm not seeing this correctly." So the way to redeem it, and it has to done seventy times seven sometimes, you go within and ask to see the person clearly (although Joel said that is cheating, but that is where we are so we will have to cheat a little bit), ask to see the person clearly or ask to be forgiven for seeing incorrectly.

If you have a problem with forgiveness, you are going to have this same facet of your consciousness appearing over and over and over again seemingly in the guise of other people. You can leave a job where you had a problem with a supervisor or coworker and think that by leaving that job you are going to get away from this thing. You take a new job, perhaps in a new city, and within a month or two there it is again. So being on a spiritual path we know "Ok, this is something that has got to be redeemed in my consciousness; there is nobody out there who keeps appearing to me. I'm the one taking this with me wherever I go."

We begin, if we are at this place, by forgiving. "Father forgive him for he knows not what he does." And over and over and over and over and over, any time that person appears to you, you keep forgiving and if you are high enough in consciousness, you realize you are only forgiving yourself. But a secret Joel gave us is there can be no forgiveness until there is absolutely no chance that we might commit that same error again. When that error is completely forgiven in our consciousness, then forgiveness occurs. This, though, is the process we go through: loving our neighbor as ourselves, understanding there is no person out there for me to forgive. This is the mirror of my mind reflecting to me myself, my concept of myself, not my real Self, my false concepts of myself. And I'm standing in front of that mirror and there it is and no matter how I try to get away from it, every time I walk in front of that mirror there it is. So that is what I mean by redemption. Redeeming these false states, these false qualities or facets of human consciousness, restores that energy to its original pure state. There are many ways that come to us in which to practice redemption, but forgiveness is the most important.

My mother taught me when I was a little girl that the surest way to make friends with your neighbor was to borrow a cup of sugar. She said "It is an interesting thing, that when you ask someone for help, it breaks the ice and you become friends." I've never forgotten this. You might want to practice when you are at odds with somebody to ask them for help. It is not the highest state of consciousness, but it certainly helps you to see differently and the response is usually beautiful. It always has been when I've tried it.

Q: *When a claim comes to me for healing, is it my duty to handle this claim alone or should I pass the claim along to my teacher or the practitioners' group?*

A: The claim has come to you. The *I* of your being is the *I* of your teacher's being and the *I* of the practitioner's being; when a claim comes to you for healing—if someone asks you for help, and I assume this is what that question means—it is not your duty to handle it, it is your privilege to handle it. You are having your Christhood recognized and if you say "I will refer you to my teacher or practitioner," you are denying your own Christhood. So your response is "Yes, I will be glad to. Yes, I can help you. Yes, I will take care of this," and then you turn from the appearance, go within—maybe terrified—but do it. Go within. You cannot say no, not if you want to move along the path. You cannot say no, and you go within and you are still, and you wait, and then you feel the release or you feel the Presence and the work is done.

Then if that claim comes back to you in two hours or three hours, you do the same thing again. This is as we had yesterday, healing beyond words and thoughts. First, we know the letter of truth and we use that and apply that to every conceivable thing in our everyday life. Then comes the knowledge that the spirit of truth has taken over and spirit is invisible. But remember what we had: Faith is the evidence of things unseen. Our faith will make us whole. So when we are called upon, we feel this Presence or have this deep breath or a flooding of consciousness, however it comes, and when it does, it is something extraordinary. It is something different from what you experience in your daily human lives. You know it's fourth-dimensional. Then comes our trust: it is done. It is finished. Then we go on about our business.

When the claim hits our consciousness again, we go back and do the same thing, but never praying to heal somebody, never even concerning ourselves with a healing. All we are interested in doing is "turning ye" from the appearance to the Spirit, closing our eyes, turning away from the mirror, closing our eyes, being still, and letting the Christ of our own consciousness do the work.

Now that is spiritual healing. It is also spiritual healing, as I was just telling you about the intellect, to realize "Well this has no power over me—I'm walking away from it." That is being the truth do you see? That is when I am the truth. "You have no power over me, what do I have to do about this? Nothing." If somebody tells you a lie and you know it's a lie, you're not going to do anything about it. You just smile to yourself and say "That's a lie," and go on. You don't fight it, you don't resist it. You just know it's a lie. And that is being the truth, that is being conscious of the truth, and what you are conscious of is what you are.

So, be very careful that you realize this with no pride and no ego, that this is a recognition of your Christhood. It is an opportunity, and "you may not pass by on the other side."*

Q: *If a student is aware of a claim of illness or lack in a friend, family member, or business associate, is it an error to take them into our meditation?*

A: No, of course not. If you are disturbed by the appearance, if you can't see through the illusion of illness regardless of who it is—even if it is someone you pass on the street—then it becomes your work to clear your own consciousness. We must understand we are never working with people. We are never working even with claims. We are working with our own consciousness of Truth. There is no truth in the human scene. There is no truth in intellect. There is no truth in any of these appearances. All appearances are lies. The illusion is when we get sucked into believing them—the hypnotist's tricks which would make us believe that there is a white poodle sitting at our feet or that we are eating ice cream when we are eating meat. That is hypnotism. And so, when we look at an individual who appears to be sick or dying, that is an illusion, and depending on our ability to realize this, there will be an instantaneous healing, there might be a healing that takes two weeks and sometimes no healing at all. But here again there are factors behind the scenes that we won't get into at this time, but there are factors that depend on the response of the individual who is showing forth the appearance.

I have had healings take place among my husband's friends, some with serious claims, who have no idea what

---

* Refer to Recording 0562B: World Work 1964 – "We May Not Pass By on the Other Side." Available for purchase from www.joelgoldsmith. com.

kind of work I do. They will call in the evening after they've seen him in the daytime. I'll answer the phone and they'll say "Meg, I just wanted Harry to know that I'm going into the hospital tomorrow," or "Meg, I just wanted Harry to know that I'm going to stay home tomorrow because I'm not feeling well." They don't ask to speak to Harry, they just tell me. Later, I hear from Harry, "You know John had surgery today and did real well." Or "So and so was ill and got over it quickly."

One friend of Harry's had been given three months to live with terminal cancer. Harry took him to the hospital one Monday morning for an x-ray and he was there over five hours. Monday evening, Harry came in, worn out from being at the hospital which drags him down with depression—all these people dying. I asked, "What's the matter?" and he said, "Well I'm just worn out from being there all day." I said, "How is John?" "Oh, he's fine, he's up, the doctors gave him a reprieve. He said, 'The cancer's been arrested.'" I asked, "What does that mean?" Harry replied, "I don't know. It means it hasn't grown any, that it won't kill him now, but it might kill him later. That means he can stay through the Super Bowl." Interestingly enough, this is the question this man asked the doctor three weeks ago. "I really want to make it through the Super Bowl." He is a football addict, so the doctor said, "Well I can't promise you that," but do you see? This man has arrested his own cancer so he can get through the Super Bowl. He's up and Harry's down in the dumps.

What I'm trying to say is that anyone who hits up against your consciousness with an erroneous claim, if you are living in this Spirit, if you are living in this consciousness, you don't have to do anything. You just have to recognize, and a lot of healings take place that you never even know about that you have been an instrument for. As you live this life, even if it is just a trip to the supermarket, make your contact before you leave home so that you go as a blessing. This is another discipline.

Whenever I get into my car, I start the engine and I sit there for a few moments and make my contact so that I'm sure that wherever I'm going I'm going as a blessing. As you are aware of this, you will have a beautiful response from the people all around you in the places that you go. But here again, "Choose ye." Where you have dominion, what you are doing is filling your mind with truth. Now since you know what your mind is, and you are filling it with truth, what can reflect back to you? This is the principle. But if you fill your mind with judgment and envy and malice and hurt feelings and self-indulgence, then that is what is going to reflect back to you. If you're aggressive, egotistical, avaricious, these are going to reflect back to you. And so human beings just keep complaining over and over and over again about their lot in life and how people are so hateful and what do they do? They seek out other people who have the same state of conscious-ness. Misery loves company. Okay?

But so do angels. Angels love company. Those on a spiri-tual path seek each other out. The work that we do, our spiri-tual purpose and function and being in this incarnation, is for service to God through service to humankind. Do you know every individual has a spiritual purpose? Every individual is here to perform a spiritual ministry. No one is excluded. But most especially, those who are on a spiritual path have come prepared to do this work. It is when we refuse or we delay, or we think we are inadequate or we are mentally lazy, or allow our attention to be drawn outward to the things of this world, then we are failing our initiation. We are refusing to do the work we came here to do.

Once again, we return to spiritual supply; our motivation is very important to the demonstration of spiritual supply. Now when we do healing work, especially for those people who do not have any idea what we are doing, can you not see what a beautifully spiritually motivated ministry that is? You all have had the opportunity to work with the practitioners' group today. These people are un-selfed. They work every day together—on world claims, community claims, anything that comes in through the newspapers, the television, anything that the students bring to them, anything that I bring to them. They are completely impersonal. Now do you think the community knows what they are doing? Or even cares? Yet the community benefits from this; this is an unsung work; a spiritual ministry is an unsung work. The few people who really understand it express gratitude in the ultimate way, through their own inner consciousness of God appearing as humankind. So when that awareness is attained, that is the highest expression of gratitude. That is the highest expression of supply. This is what this practitioners' group does every day; they realize and know the truth about you and about me and the community and the state and the world. That is their highest spiritual motivation and they are asking for nothing back. They don't have to ask for anything back. They have no needs. They know the principle of spiritual supply.

This, you see, is tithing in its ultimate sense. When we share our material goods, even if we don't understand the spiritual principle behind it, that level of consciousness is where we start. Even in churches people tithe, and with many they tithe thinking they are going to get something back. Now when you tithe spiritually, you are completely out of your sense of your little self, such as this group. Tithing is done here because the principle is understood that all that the

Father has is mine, and that I can give nothing to anybody else. It is never a question of giving because somebody needs. It is a totally different motivation. It is a giving and a sharing because *I* have. And this is my spiritual activity, you see?

In other words, without that spontaneous spiritual grasp of the motivation of the reason you are doing this, then your act does not carry the power or the force to return to you your own. In other words, as long as you think *you* are doing something, then you are denying your own Godhood because you and I don't even have the capacity to give to each other do you see? Whereas if we understand "I and the Father are one and all that the Father has is mine" and I can never give everything because it is infinite, in that knowledge, that state of consciousness, we know that nothing belongs to us; then we can freely give and freely receive because it is all of the Father. That is spiritual motivation and so your supply then is unlimited. As long as you are an instrument through which this comes, you don't have to think about it coming back; if you are spiritually endowed with that wisdom, it just flows. When individuals are spiritually motivated in the sharing, then it is pure consciousness doing that sharing and the form can be multiplied.

Any form is based on pure consciousness, spiritual consciousness. That consciousness becomes the essence, and like the loaves and the fishes can be multiplied; images in the mind cannot. So spontaneous spiritual sharing is the ultimate of tithing, never looking for a return because you know you don't need a return. How could you need a return if it is you who are the giver? And it is a fascinating and interesting thing that the more you expand your capacity or the more your capacity to give is expanded, the greater is your capacity to receive. But it is not only material goods that we should be interested in.

Let's take our first group leader's presentation that was presented yesterday.* His beautiful spiritual motivation to share created an organ into which all of us can express, share ourselves, with no thought of anything coming back to us right? This is just a beautiful expression of love to anyone who wants to participate, to contribute to, and to anyone who wants to read what is put into that periodical. This group leader will be doing all of the work of laying it out and printing it and making it available. This is his act of love, as your articles are acts of love, just to share.

Now in this instance, we can see that. When we share material goods, something happens to our consciousness. But there has to be an overall acceptance of a spiritual principle. Otherwise you are a house divided and every time you write a check you think you are giving something of your own to somebody or you are paying a bill. But the true expression of gratitude is every time you write a check at all, you should inwardly express gratitude for having that capacity to do so. Always. And never hold back. Because you know now that any time you hold back you are the one who is being held back. If you don't pay your bills, who are you not paying? Yourself. And so your income will be slower and slower coming in.

Q: *Please explain what is done if this person asks directly for a healing versus being made aware of the claim either through a third party or direct observation.*

A: Of course, we have just gone through that. You say, "yes." Now being made aware through direct observation, we

---

* The first workshop leader of the workshop portion of the class, created a group project whereby class participants would share ongoing written inspirations, or vignettes, which were compiled into a continuing publication.

just covered. Being made aware of the claim through a third party, I suppose this student means somebody has gossiped. "Did you hear that so and so is sick?" Well, that's a rumor, and once again, who told you this? How do you know this is true? I have attended people who claim to be very ill and who look perfectly wonderful to me. So that is a rumor. And if I accept that as the truth, then what happens? I take the claim on. The minute that I set myself up to heal you of something, I believe you've got it. And since there is only one Consciousness, I'm taking that claim on.

It is easier when the rumor comes to you through television or the newspaper or a third party to just reject it. "This is not true, I have no evidence this is true." That is simple to do. But when someone asks you directly, then you do the work. All of this depends on your reaction. The secret of healing is in non-reaction. If you react, if you think there is something to be healed, if you think that there is work to be done, then you are the one in trouble and it is you that needs the healing. So again we go within, ask to have our consciousness cleared, to see this as it really is; we turn from the appearance. Never, never, ask for a healing. That is praying amiss and you won't get it. So it is always your consciousness you are working with; it is always you who needs the work.

Q: There is another question here: *I need to clarify how the mind is used. I understand the mind to be a storage place, a kind of library of images; the mind processes from the intellect. The mind is the instrument through which the Spirit flows. Is this correct? The intellect is the human ego. This is what has to be re-programmed to know the truth. Am I headed in the right direction?*

A: Well it would take a whole other class to go through this again, but I suggest that you study the transcripts on the

Mind and the Intellect which all of you have, and also get the tapes that we have made and really work with these.[*] I think that is it for tonight.

Thank you.

---

[*] Refer to Recordings 9403A&B; 9494 A&B – "Mind and Intellect" series with Margaret Johnson.

For more information on
Margaret Johnson's work contact:

www.mysticsoftheworld.com
publishing@mysticsoftheworld.com